Selling Spirituality

From feng shui to holistic medicine, from aromatherapy candles to yoga weekends, spirituality is big business. It promises to soothe away the angst of modern living, and to offer an antidote to shallow materialism. *Selling Spirituality* is a short, sharp attack on this fallacy.

It shows how spirituality has in fact become a powerful commodity in the global marketplace – a cultural addiction that reflects orthodox politics, curbs self-expression and colonises Eastern beliefs. Exposing how spirituality has today come to embody the privatisation of religion in the modern West, **Jeremy Carrette** and **Richard King** reveal the people and brands who profit from this corporate hijack, and explore how spirituality can be reconfigured as a means of resistance to capitalism and its deceptions.

Jeremy Carrette teaches at the University of Kent at Canterbury, UK, and was formerly Head of Religious Studies at the University of Stirling, and is author of *Foucault and Religion* (2000). **Richard King** is a scholar of Indian philosophy and religion and has taught in several British universities. He is the author of three previous books including *Orientalism and Religion* (1999) and currently lives and writes in Paris.

JEREMY CARRETTE
AND RICHARD KING

Selling
Spirituality
The silent takeover
of religion

Routledge
Taylor & Francis Group

LONDON AND NEW YORK

First published 2005
by Routledge,
2 Park Square, Milton Park, Abingdon, Oxon, OX14 4RN

Simultaneously published in the USA and Canada
by Routledge
270 Madison Ave, New York, NY 10016

Routledge is an imprint of the Taylor & Francis Group

Transferred to Digital Printing 2005

Typeset in Joanna MT by
RefineCatch Ltd, Bungay, Suffolk

British Library Cataloguing in Publication Data
A catalogue record for this book is available from the British Library

Library of Congress Cataloging in Publication Data
Carrette, Jeremy R.
  Selling spirituality : the silent takeover of religion /
  Jeremy Carrette and Richard King.—1st ed.
  Includes bibliographical references and index.
  1. Spiritual life. I. King, Richard, 1966– II. Title.
  BL624.C3475 2004
  204—dc22
                                              2004005324

ISBN 0-415-30208-0 (hbk)
ISBN 0-415-30209-9 (pbk)

For Florence, Cécile, and Lila

Contents

Acknowledgements

And it is possible that, in the realm of human destiny, the depth of man's questioning is more important than his answers.

André Malraux, *Anti-Memoirs* [1967], Penguin, 1970, p. 15

This book emerged out of a profound discomfort with the way in which neoliberalism, ostensibly a capitalist economic theory emerging in the late twentieth century, is being presented to the post-Cold War world as the only way forward in an age of globalisation. It is a response to the increasing encroachment of the ideology of 'market forces' and utilitarian efficiency into all aspects of human culture and thought (what one might call the marketisation or commodification of life itself). It is part of the broader argument of this book that this process, precipitated by the unfettering of global financial markets in the late twentieth century, is increasingly framing the very grounds of cultural expression itself – in most cases without the conscious knowledge or consent of society as a whole. This is the silent take-over that we are attempting to expose within this work. The book originally arose from a series of conversations emerging from the authors' wider academic work in the history of religious ideas and is part of an ongoing conversation. As such, it brings together insights from cultural and social theory, the history of psychology, the study of Asian philosophies, postcolonial theory and our mutual interest in the politics of knowledge. While working on our respective long-term academic projects, both authors became fascinated by the explosion of literature on spirituality, not only in the 'mind, body, and spirit' section of bookstores but also in the various professions. Initially this book was going to be a critical introduction to that concept, but increasingly over a year of meetings it came to take on a more direct political edge. In the attempt to speak to a wider audience we have deliberately sought to approach the topic through a more accessible genre than traditional academic monographs. The book seeks to raise a series of questions in a narrative style that is more open-ended and provocative than traditional academic discourse normally allows. It is written in the spirit of the French popular *essai* and hopes to speak to wider political concerns and constituencies than are usually appealed to in scholarly works.

Selling Spirituality examines the growing commercialisation of 'religion' in the form of the popular notion of 'spirituality', as it is found in education, health-care, counselling, business training, management theory and marketing. The analysis offered is but one example of the way in which the 'market mentality' is now infiltrating all aspects of human cultural expression in (so-called) 'advanced' capitalist societies. The book provides a critical philosophical discussion of issues arising from this contemporary cultural shift in relation to the spheres of religion and spirituality, but does not attempt to provide an exhaustive overview of the various groups and literature concerned. Rather, the book seeks to address the politics of knowledge surrounding the idea of spirituality and draw attention to the pernicious social effects of neoliberalism and the corporate takeover of society that such shifts represent. The work is an explicitly political project in that it seeks to challenge the commodification of life as well as disrupt the domestication of diverse cultural traditions, practices and communities in terms of an increasingly homogenised, sanitised and socially pacifying conception of spirituality. In writing such a book, we hope to raise awareness of the ways in which popular discourses about 'spirituality' tend to displace questions of social justice, being increasingly framed by the individualist and corporatist values of a consumer society.

We would like to thank a number of people for supporting this project. In particular, Roger Thorp, then Routledge commissioning editor for religion in the UK, for trusting us enough to make this project a viable concern, and Clare Johnson for following it through its various stages. We would also like to thank John I'Anson of the Department of Education at Stirling University for providing references to material on education and spirituality. Richard would like to make special mention of the University of Derby, UK, for making him personally aware of the effects of market forces in the workplace and for providing a case study of the transformation of university education into a retail enterprise. We would like to thank Richard Roberts and two anonymous reviewers for their constructive and critical comments, Wendy Pearce for useful references on business and spirituality and Jude and Richard Fox for useful clarifications. Jeremy would like to thank Ron McKechnie and the New Directions in the Study of Alcohol Group for inviting him to speak at the 25th Annual Conference in Dumfries, Scotland, in April 2001, on the topic of spirituality and addiction, which formed the basis for some of the work. Such an event provided rich insights into the increasing use of spirituality by healthcare practitioners and was a creative forum for exploring the issues. We would also like to thank Tim Carrette for engaging us with his understanding of the value of 'spirituality' and for challenging our own political reading of the material. We hope that we have refined our arguments sufficiently in the light of your questions. Thanks also to Vicki Clifford for letting Jeremy use her cottage to finish his writing and to Paulette and Jean-Claude Faucher for providing Richard and Florence with a home, a place to work and plenty of good food and Bordeaux wine, both in Paris and Le Teich. A special thanks to Paulette for access to her private collection of books on spirituality.

This book was written intermittently during a year of enormous change in the personal and political spaces of our lives and reflects many enjoyable weekends in Derby, Paris and Edinburgh. Jeremy would like to thank Cécile for all her love and magical times together in Paris, London and Worcester College, Oxford, which have forever changed his life. Thanks to Florence for making it possible for 'strangers to meet in the night' and Anne-Marie for providing us with a place for 'dancing in the rain' until we found our own home. Richard would like to thank Florence for her love and support, particularly through the last three years of breathtaking change and stress in both of their lives, and for enriching his life with her love, smile and companionship. Both authors wish to express their gratitude to Florence not only for her friendship but also for her critical acumen in reading and commenting on various drafts of this work. If this book succeeds in being accessible at all, that is a testament to Florence's careful proofreading. Thanks also to little Lila for reminding her father of the importance of changing nappies and giving cuddles as well as taking a stand for the sake of future generations.

Jeremy Carrette and Richard King,
February 2004

Spirituality and the Rebranding of Religion
Introduction

God is dead but has been resurrected as 'Capital'.

From feng shui to holistic medicine, from aromatherapy candles to yoga weekends, from Christian mystics to New Age gurus, spirituality is big business. There has been an explosion of interest and popular literature on mind, body and spirit and 'personal development'. We now see the introduction of modes of 'spirituality' into educational curricula, bereavement and addiction counselling, psychotherapy and nursing. Spirituality as a cultural trope has also been appropriated by corporate bodies and management consultants to promote efficiency, extend markets and maintain a leading edge in a fast-moving information economy. For many people, spirituality has replaced religion as old allegiances and social identities are transformed by modernity. However, in a context of individualism and erosion of traditional community allegiances, 'spirituality' has become a new cultural addiction and a claimed panacea for the angst of modern living. Spirituality is celebrated by those who are disillusioned by traditional institutional religions and seen as a force for wholeness, healing and inner transformation. In this sense spirituality is taken to denote the positive aspects of the ancient religious traditions, unencumbered by the 'dead hand' of the Church, and yet something which provides a liberation and solace in an otherwise meaningless world. But is this emergence of the idea of spirituality all that it seems? Is something more complex and suspicious at work in the glorification of the spiritual?

To contest some of the dominant readings of 'spirituality' within western societies and their silencing of traditions will require some examination of how these discourses operate in the contemporary socio-economic world. This book emerges from a frustration with the lack of clarity and critical discussion of the concept of spirituality, a notion that has become pervasive in contemporary society in the consciousness of its advocates and its detractors. The concept therefore represents on the one hand all that is banal and vague about New Age religiosity, while on the other signifying a transcendent quality, enhancing life and distilling all that is positive from the 'ageing and outdated' casks of traditional religious institutions.

This book attempts to uncover what amounts to a silent takeover of 'the religious' by contemporary capitalist ideologies by means of the increasingly popular discourse of 'spirituality'. We seek to challenge the contemporary use of this concept as a means of reflecting and supporting social and economic policies geared towards the neo-liberal ideals of privatisation and corporatisation, applied increasingly to all spheres of human life.

QUESTIONING MODERN SPIRITUALITY

What is neoliberalism and what exactly does it have to do with spirituality?

> Neoliberalism is the defining political economic paradigm of our time – it refers to the policies and processes whereby a relative handful of private interests are permitted to control as much as possible of social life in order to maximise their personal profit. Associated initially with Reagan and Thatcher, neoliberalism has for the past two decades been the dominant global political economic trend adopted by political parties of the center, much of the traditional left, and the right. These parties and the policies they enact represent the immediate interests of extremely wealthy investors and less than one thousand large corporations.
>
> (McChesney, 1999: 8)

For many, spirituality would seem to have little to do with questions of economics and politics. The roots of this modern attitude go back to eighteenth century European thought (the Enlightenment), where the underlying principles of liberalism were born. In challenging the traditional social, moral and philosophical authority of the Church, European intellectuals sought to establish a framework for society and politics that avoided the religious conflicts of previous centuries. The solution, outlined most notably by philosophers such as John

Locke, was to relegate the religious to the private sphere of life – to clearly demarcate it from the public realms of politics, science and philosophy.

The Enlightenment is also a period characterised by attempts to define the specificity of these different aspects of cultural life. This led to an intellectual obsession with defining the precise characteristics of religion (a preoccupation that continues to this day). This is a misleading enterprise because it takes conceptual distinctions with a specific history of their own and treats them as if they are features of the world rather than of a culturally specific way of understanding it. It is clear for instance that it makes little sense to draw a sharp distinction between the secular (politics, economics, science, philosophy) and the religious dimensions of human life in any other culture than those conditioned by modern liberalism and the European Enlightenment philosophies of the eighteenth century. We should also make our position on this question clear from the start: *There is no essence or definitive meaning to terms like spirituality or religion.* The attraction of defining an essence is that it clearly demarcates a field for the purposes of analysis. Such a move, however, leaves the impression that spirituality is some-how *really* divorced from other spheres of human life such as economics, culture and politics. The desire to attribute a universal essence to the meaning of spirituality also ignores the historical and cultural traces and differences in the uses of the term. Searching for an over-arching definition of 'spirituality' only ends up missing the specific historical location of each use of the term. There is no view from nowhere – no Archimedian point outside of history – from which one could determine a fixed and universal meaning for the term 'spirituality'.

This book seeks to shift debate about religion and spirituality away from a misleading emphasis upon truth and authenticity ('What counts as real spirituality?') towards a consideration of the socio-political consequences of such claims ('Who benefits from particular constructions of "spirituality"?'). Our approach is to pay attention, following William James, to the 'fruits not the roots' of contemporary uses of the term. What are the socio-political effects of the decision to classify specific practices or philosophies as 'spiritual' and who benefits from such constructions? However, where we differ from James – a primary exponent of a psychological definition of religious experience – is in wishing to displace the individualisation of the spiritual, since it is precisely this which has allowed consumerist and capitalist spiritualities to emerge in the late twentieth century.

There are two features of this relatively new phenomenon that we seek to contest. First, we wish to challenge constructions of spirituality that promote the subsuming of the ethical and the religious in terms of an overriding economic agenda. We do not do this out of some attempt to privilege some pure realm known as 'the religious' or 'the spiritual' and separate it from apparently 'worldly' concerns. In our view there is no distinct realm known as 'the religious' that exists in isolation from the social, political and economic world (King, 1999a; Carrette, 2000). This is not to reduce 'the religious' out of existence but to refuse to isolate it from those other dimensions of human life (except for the purposes of analysis). There may be no pure *homo religiosus* but there is also no *homo oeconomicus*, despite the increasing dominance of the economic as an apparent indicator of fundamental human motivation and action.

Those traditions classified as 'religions' in the modern consciousness have always been bound up with economics and modes of exchange. However, a fundamental ground shift has taken place in American and British culture in the last twenty years, related to the deregulation of the markets by Ronald Reagan and Margaret Thatcher in the 1980s, and this is changing the relationship of cultural forms to the market. With the development of organisations like the World Trade Organisation (WTO) and the emergence of neoliberalism as the dominant economic ideology of our time, this cultural and political shift has already gone global. With the emergence of capitalist spirituality we are seeing an attempted takeover by a specific economic agenda of the cultural space traditionally inhabited by 'the religions'. Entering public institutions that provide education, healthcare and professional expertise within society as a whole, the ideologies of consumerism and business enterprise are now infiltrating more and more aspects of our lives. The result of this shift has been an erasure of the wider social and ethical concerns associated with religious traditions and communities and the subordination of 'the religious' and the ethical to the realm of economics, which is now rapidly replacing science (just as science replaced theology in a previous era), as the dominant mode of authoritative discourse within society.

This represents the second feature of dominant conceptions of spirituality that we wish to challenge and this is their essentially accommodationist orientation. In a sense, the most troubling aspect of many modern spiritualities is precisely that they are not troubling enough. They promote

> 'The danger is that religion could become no more than a service sector to the global civilization, no longer shaping its values but merely repairing the spiritual damage it inflicts.'
>
> Harvey Cox, 'Christianity', in Mark Juergensmeyer (ed.), *Global Religions: An Introduction*, Oxford University Press, 2003, p. 24.

accommodation to the social, economic and political mores of the day and provide little in terms of a challenge to the status quo or to a lifestyle of self-interest and ubiquitous consumption.

One response to the emergence of capitalist spirituality might be to argue that this is not 'true' or real spirituality. Such a move would imply that there is something easily identifiable as 'spiritual' in the world that would correspond to the real or proper usage of the term. In any case, whose construction of the term are we to take as the normative standard by which all others are to be judged? Rather, we wish to challenge the individualist and corporatist monopoly of the term spirituality and the cultural space that this demarcates at the beginning of the twenty-first century for the promotion of the values of consumerism and corporate capitalism. We do this, not because we wish to appeal to some kind of ancient 'authentic' or 'true' spirituality to which they do not conform (as if that or any definition could encompass the historical phenomena captured by the diverse uses of the term 'spirituality'), but rather to open up a contested space that will allow alternative, more socially engaged, constructions of the term to express themselves.

What is being sold to us as radical, trendy and transformative spirituality in fact produces little in the way of a significant change in one's lifestyle or fundamental behaviour patterns (with the possible exception of motivating the individual to be more efficient and productive at work). By 'cornering the market' on spirituality, such trends actually limit the socially transformative dimensions of the religious perspectives that they draw upon by locating 'the spiritual' firmly within a privatised and conformist space. Sadly, not only have the primary exponents of 'the spiritual' generally failed to address this issue, but academic commentators upon these new forms of spirituality, even when noticing such trends, have generally preferred the language of so-called 'neutral description' rather than that of cultural critique. Most have emphasised the 1960s and 1970s context, and ignored the spread of market ideology within culture in the 1980s and 1990s. What we have seen emerge in the last few decades of the twentieth century has been a form of 'New Age Capitalism' (Lau, 2000) and it offers a fundamental challenge to our global cultural heritage that it is in the process of colonising.

CULTURE AS NETWORK: SOCIAL PATTERNS AND THOUGHT-CONTROL

As critics such as Karl Marx pointed out long ago, those traditions that we now classify as 'religions' (but which in the past simply amounted to the dominant cosmologies and civilisations of their time), have always provided a means of controlling the thought-processes of people, if only because of their ideologically privileged position within society. To apply Marx's critical eye to the religions, but then to fail to observe the development of new institutions of thought-control in so-called modern 'secular' societies, is to take our eyes off the ball and become too attached to Marx's emphasis upon 'the religions' as opiates of the masses. To follow Marx in his analysis is to go beyond him (Maduro, 1977). The rise of capitalist spirituality is a manifestation of a wider process of cultural shifts (and forms of 'thought-control'), linked to what Noam Chomsky has called 'the control of the public mind', and is associated with the rise of new institutions and dominant ideologies within society. The most striking feature of our brave new world is the emergence of large multinational corporations (many of which are economically more powerful than most nation-states), and the rise in the 1990s of an economic orthodoxy within the post-war Bretton Woods institutions (such as the IMF and the World Bank) that sought to extend the Thatcherite/Reaganite agendas but on a global scale. The so-called 'Washington Consensus' that has emerged, consolidated by the establishment of unelected organisations such as the World Trade Organisation (WTO, founded in 1995), remains intent upon promoting a global deregulation of markets (euphemistically called 'free trade'), an ideology of unfettered global consumption ('continued economic growth') and the privatisation of public assets and services ('ending state-owned monopolies'; 'introducing market competitiveness and business efficiency to health, education, transport, media, etc.').

In the political, cultural and ideological space evacuated by the collapse of the Berlin Wall in 1989, a triumphalist form of corporate capitalism has emerged with a new cadre of powerful leaders and institutions seeking to promote its spread. The new economic and political orthodoxy in this emerging world order is known as neoliberalism and it puts profits before people, promotes privatisation of public utilities, services and resources, and is in the process of eroding many of the individual civil liberties that were established under

> Of the 100 largest economies in the world, 51 are corporations; only 49 are countries.
>
> While the sales of the Top 200 corporations are the equivalent of 27.5% of world economic activity, they employ only 0.78% of the world's workforce.
>
> The Top 200's combined sales are 18 times the size of the combined annual income of the 1.2 billion people (24% of the total world population) living in 'severe' poverty.
>
> Report of the Institute of Policy Studies, New York, 2000.

its forerunner – political liberalism. The rights once given to individuals and enshrined in historic documents like the American Bills of Rights and the French Declaration of Human Rights (1789) are now being displaced by an ideology that sees everything (and we mean *everything*) as a commodity that can be bought and sold and which promotes corporate rights over respect for individual and community rights. Recently, for instance, in response to a legal challenge to the alleged mendacity of their own publicity about workers' conditions, we have seen Nike argue in US courts that the American right to free speech applies to corporations as much as to individuals and that they have the right to express their own views about themselves (*Guardian*, 23 June 2003). Similarly, in 2004 we find 'yoga entrepreneurs' such as Bikram Choudhury, a former weightlifter based in Los Angeles, asserting copyright ownership of a set of yoga postures. According to the the *Guardian*:

> Mr Choudhury has sent letters to more than 100 Bikram yoga schools and teachers, accusing them of violating his copyright and trademark by deviating from his strict teachings and employing instructors who were not trained by him. In response, a collective of US yoga teachers are suing Mr Choudhury in a San Francisco federal court, arguing that his copyright and trademark claims are unenforceable, because his teachings draw on postures that have been in public use for centuries. 'No one can own a style of yoga,' James Harrison, a lawyer for the collective said.
>
> (*Guardian*, 9 February 2004)

In response to creeping marketisation and the emergence of neo-liberalism as the dominant ideology of globalisation in our era we have seen the rise of a coalition of groups, of various shades and creeds, that have been labelled variously as 'anti-capitalist', 'anti-globalisation' or, to use the French expression, 'alter-mondialiste'. Despite their great diversity, what tends to unite these movements is their resistance to the spread of neoliberal ideology, as summed up in the slogan: 'The World Is Not For Sale'. Whereas twentieth-century politics was dominated by competition between 'the Left' and 'the Right', it is likely that the twenty-first century will bring new reconfigurations that will emerge from this tension between corporate-driven globalisation and community-driven internationalism. As Leslie Sklair (2002: 277) notes,

> the real distinction [is] between diametrically opposed beliefs based on entirely different conceptions of the satisfaction of human needs, between the quest for the good life promoted by capitalist globalization and the quest for the good society at the base of the radical alternatives to capitalist globalization. This is one of the central issues around which the embryonic anti-globalization movement is coming

together as it emerges out of protectionism, new social movements and Green movements.

Of course, as the conservative American commentator Thomas Friedman (2000: 164) admits, the world of business cannot flourish without the support of the state and the military in particular:

> The hidden hand of the market will never work without a hidden fist. Markets function and flourish only when property rights are secured and can be enforced, which in turn requires a political framework protected and backed by military power . . . Indeed, McDonalds cannot flourish without McDonnell Douglas, the designer of the US Air Force F-15. And the hidden fist that keeps the world safe for Silicon Valley's technologies to flourish is called the US Army, Air Force, Navy and Marine Corps.

Military force of course is not enough to impose any belief-system or ideology upon a population. One also needs, as Chomsky reminds us, to 'manufacture consent' and encourage complicity, whether consciously or unwittingly, among key institutions and groups within society. This requires the involvement of educational institutions, communications and media providers and a whole host of professional organisations (representing 'authoritative knowledge' and 'specialist expertise') to mould public perceptions of reality. It is in this broader context that we would like to explore within this book the ways in which professional organisations (education, healthcare, counselling, business) within western societies have become increasingly interested in the notion of 'spirituality'.

> In the democratic system, the necessary illusions cannot be imposed by force. Rather, they must be instilled in the public mind by more subtle means . . . Debate cannot be stilled, and indeed, in a properly functioning system of propaganda, it should not be, because it has a system-reinforcing character if constrained within proper bounds. What is essential is to set the bounds firmly. Controversy may rage as long as it adheres to the presuppositions that define the consensus of elites, and it should furthermore be encouraged within these bounds, thus helping to establish these doctrines as the very

condition of thinkable thought while reinforcing the belief that freedom reigns.

(Chomsky, 1989: 48)

How exactly do ideas control people? In order to understand how we see 'spirituality' in general functioning as a political and economic concept, it is necessary to move beyond mainstream ways of thinking about religious ideas –

> 'The most potent weapon of the oppressor is the mind of the oppressed.'
>
> Steve Biko, *I Write What I Like: A Selection of His Writings*, ed. Aelred Stubbs, Rand Press, 1996.

ideas that we have been taught in our schools and universities and through the media. Culture is a dynamic network of relations that can never be adequately represented by fixed categories such as 'religion', 'politics', 'economics', etc., even though people often use these terms as if they refer to distinct spheres of human life. For analytic purposes such distinctions can be useful in order to separate out aspects of intricate cultural phenomena from the wider cultural network in which they operate. We should not be fooled however into believing that these abstractions somehow directly mirror the complexity of culture itself. When we use terms like 'religion', 'politics' and 'economics' the impression can be created that these are autonomous realms of human cultural experience, which bear little or no relation to each other. In reality, of course, all of these dimensions of human life form a complex network of relations. We are led to compartmentalise in this way partly because modern liberalism (deriving from the Enlightenment) has encouraged us to fear the mixture of politics and religion and promoted in its place a model of the modern secular state where religion is safely kept at the margins of society or in the minds of its individual members. As a result, we are peculiarly predisposed to see religion, economics and politics as separate domains of the social world. Any detailed analysis of human history will soon demonstrate, however, that this is a gross over-simplification.

We are all predisposed to see the world according to a set of inherited cultural habits, embodied practices and thought forms (what Bourdieu called 'habitus'). Patterns of thinking emerge in the social world that prevent people from seeing both the interconnections of culture and power and also the ability of ideas to disrupt and challenge the established order. Moreover, most of us, even if at times reluctantly and with considerable cynicism, tend to accept the picture of the social world presented to us by the mass media, the state apparatus and our educational systems, because we are simply trying to cope with the everyday struggles of life. As Robert Bellah notes in *The Good Society* (1992), there is widespread disillusionment within contemporary western societies and a growing sense of disempowerment with regard to the operations of the major institutions that govern our lives. Moreover, he argues, the rugged individualism of the new market-oriented society encourages citizens to lose themselves in private pursuits and pleasures, allowing the major institutions of government and the economy to operate 'over our heads' without proper democratic accountability.

Since humans have a basic need for security and a sense of certainty about how the world is constructed, it is often easier to accept the picture of the world given to us rather than to question it. Too much questioning and change can cause anxiety. Often it is only when the basic 'comfort zone' of living is threatened, as in the face of oppression, poverty or perceived danger, that people start to protest. This reluctance to question how we think and to challenge basic assumptions means that powerful institutions are able to take the initiative in influencing and shaping the world and our conception of it.

In order to appreciate the critique offered in this book, one is required to accept two basic principles: first, that how we think is formed through interaction with the social world and its institutions; and, second, that power is exercised by a network of institutions, with the aim of directing the flow of information and shaping public perceptions of what counts as truth. In this way, members of society are conditioned – socialised is the polite word for it – to see the world in a particular way. This is what Chomsky calls 'manufacturing consent', that is the setting of limits on the very possibility of thinking. In the pre-modern period, much of this 'thought-control' at the social level was exerted by institutions such as the Church. With the emergence of the nation-state in the modern period much of the burden for conditioning the masses passed from religious institutions to state institutions through the establishment of national education systems, social welfare structures, parliament, the legislature and the various media of communication. In a contemporary context we are seeing the emergence of what Philip Bobbitt (2002) has called the 'market-state'.

> Whereas the nation-state, with its mass free public education, universal franchise, and social security policies, promised to guarantee the welfare of the nation, the market-state promises instead to maximise the opportunity of the people and thus tends to privatise many state activities and to make voting and representative government less influential and more responsive to the market.
>
> (Bobbitt, 2002: 211)

Power again is shifting (as it always does). This time, however, the institutions increasingly exerting their influence upon us are multi-national corporations, big business and the mass media (increasingly owned by those same corporations). In all cases throughout history such institutional control has resulted in various forms of resistance. Knowledge is always political and power always produces resistance.

We are never obliged to accept the dominant version of reality (however conceived throughout history) without question. As human beings we are able to challenge regimes of thought-control, but only if we become aware of them, and of the possibility of alternatives. The social world is a fermentation of attitudes and practices produced from the interaction of multiple forces that thereby constitute the social space. Information and ideas are transmitted through this social world via institutions and their public apparatus. Political, legal, educational, financial, religious and media institutions attempt to define 'truth' and inform the values through which people understand the world. These ideas and values are, of course, pushed and shaped in various ways through complex processes of social interaction. This can involve the rejection, acceptance and/or transformation of these ideas as humans live through the celebrations and struggles of being members of society. Once ideas enter the public domain they are subject to appropriation, reinterpretation and contestation by other cultural agents.

In a contemporary context the ideas and values of any given society are also subject to a series of negotiations on a global level by contact with other cultural values and ideas. The explosion of information and ideas on the internet, for example, is such that the transfer of ideas, and even money, can no longer be controlled by any single institution or nation-state. If we are now moving into a world that moves beyond the traditional boundaries of the nation-state, the rapid spread of information technology is presenting us with a new knowledge-based economy. In the new 'information age' ideas become even more important as forces of economic change and resistance. It is important to realise that change is always possible.

> Domestic and international actors reproduce or alter systems through their actions. Any given international system does not exist because of immutable structures, but rather the very structures are dependent for their reproduction on the practices of the actors. Fundamental change of the international system occurs when actors, through their practices, change the rules and norms constitutive of international interaction.
>
> (Koslowski and Kratochwil, 1994: 15)

THE TWO PHASES IN THE PRIVATISATION OF RELIGION

It is often recognised that, since the Enlightenment, 'religion' has been subjected to an erosion of its social authority with the rise of scientific rationalism, humanism and modern, liberal democratic models of the nation-state (a process often called secularisa-

> 'God is dead; but given the way of men, there may still be caves for thousands of years in which his shadow will be shown. – And we – we still have to vanquish his shadow, too.'
>
> Friedrich Nietzsche, The Gay Science [1882/1887], Vintage, 1974, p. 167.

tion). In modern western societies, to varying degrees, this has usually manifested itself as the relegation of 'the religious' to the private sphere. What has not been sufficiently appreciated by contemporary social theorists, however, is that the later stages of this process have become intimately intertwined with the global spread of corporate capitalism. We can describe both of these trends as the privatisation of religion, but in two distinct senses. In the first instance, the European Enlightenment led to an increased tendency to exclude religious discourse from the public domain of politics, economics and science. In the main this was achieved by representing 'the religious' primarily in terms of individual choice, beliefs and private states of mind. For philosophers such as John Locke and Immanuel Kant, it was important to demarcate the precise domain in which religion should be located, in order to preserve the secular space of liberal political governance from the conflicts, intolerance and violence arising from the conflict between competing religious ideologies and groups within European societies. Religion in this context becomes a matter of personal assent to a set of beliefs, a matter of the private state of mind or personal orientation of the individual citizen in the terms set out for it by modern (i.e. Enlightenment-inspired) liberalism. A consequence of this approach is that, in different ways and variegated forms, religion has been formally separated from the business of statecraft in contemporary Northern European societies (though with different inflections and degrees of smoothness). We can call this process the *individualisation* of religion.

This cultural shift has allowed a much greater degree of individual experimentation and freedom to explore religious alternatives and has been crucial in the development, for instance, of the melting-pot of religions and spiritualities that is often called the 'New Age'. The individualisation of religious sensibilities, however, has caused some to worry about the erosion of a sense of community and compassion for others in modern societies. These concerns are picked up by leading religious figures, such as the current Archbishop of Canterbury Rowan Williams, who argued in his 2002 Richard Dimbleby Lecture that

> the future of modern liberal democracies] depends heavily on those perspectives that are offered by religious belief. In the pre-modern period, religion sanctioned the social order; in the modern period it was a potential rival to be pushed to the edges, a natural reaction. But are we at the point where as the 'public sphere' becomes more value-

free, the very survival of the idea of public sphere, a realm of political
argument about vision and education, is going to demand that we take
religion a good deal more seriously
(Rowan Williams, Richard Dimbleby Lecture, 19 December 2002)

However, there are problems with Williams's understanding of
'religion'. It is already the case that the 'religious' is seeping into the
public domain of modern secular societies. First, this is occurring in
the commodification of religion as spirituality – a trend that this book
seeks to address. Second, it has entered the twenty-first century public
discourse of western nations in a violent way through the appropriation of 'Islam' by certain radical groups from the Middle East and
South Asia. Moreover, Williams does not express an awareness of the
problems in deciding what exactly counts as a 'religion'. The secular
space of modernity, that which is deemed to exclude the religious, is
itself a product of a particular 'religious' history (that of European
Christianity) and the Enlightenment reaction to it. It is also far from
clear that one can map the 'secular–religious' division onto non-
western cultures without severe distortion occurring (King, 1999a).
Nevertheless, we agree with Williams in his view that the traditional
perspectives and ethical orientations of the 'religious traditions' are
essential for the very preservation of the values of tolerance and
respect that secularism and liberalism sought to preserve in the initial
attempt to exclude the religious from the public domain.

In the late twentieth century, however, there has been a second
form of privatisation that has taken place. It partially builds upon the
previous process, but also has important discontinuities with it. It
can be characterised as a wholesale commodification of religion, that is
the selling-off of religious buildings, ideas and claims to authenticity
in service to individual/corporate profit and the promotion of a
particular worldview and mode of life, namely corporate capitalism.
Let us imagine that 'religion' in all its forms is a company that is facing
a takeover bid from a larger company known as Corporate Capitalism.
In its attempt to 'downsize' its ailing competitor, Corporate Capitalism
strips the assets of 'religion' by plundering its material and cultural
resources, which are then repackaged, rebranded and then sold in the

marketplace of ideas. This reselling exploits the historical respect and 'aura of authenticity' of the religious traditions (what in business terms is often called 'the goodwill' of the company) while at the same time, separating itself from any negative connotations associated with the religious in a modern secular context (rebranding). This is precisely the burden of the concept of spirituality in such contexts, allowing a simultaneous nod towards and separation from 'the religious'. The corporate machine or the market does not seek to validate or reinscribe the tradition but rather utilises its cultural cachet for its own purposes and profit.

Like the selling to private companies of public utilities and services in our modern neoliberal economies, such as gas, electricity, water, healthcare and transport systems, the material and cultural 'assets' of the various religious traditions are being plundered, 'downsized' and sold off as commodities. 'Religion' is facing a 'takeover bid' from the business world, without the protection of the state, which increasingly recedes from social welfare and public service initiatives in a neoliberal context. Today in most British cities you will find old church buildings that have been sold off to become business offices, supermarkets, public houses, nightclubs and private apartments. However, it is not primarily the sale of buildings that we are concerned with here, but rather the exploitation of the 'cultural capital' of the religious for the purposes of consumption and corporate gain. From the branding of perfumes using ancient Asian concepts and the idea of the spiritual ('Samsara' perfume, 'Zen' deodorant, 'Spiritual' body-spray) to clothe the product in an aura of mystical authenticity, to the promotion of management courses offering 'spiritual techniques' for the enhancement of one's work productivity and corporate business-efficiency, the sanitised religiosity of 'the spiritual' sells. However, this use of spirituality involves a number of complex levels of engagement. While appearing to endorse the values of the ancient traditions that it is

'A Religion may be discerned in capitalism – that is to say, capitalism serves essentially to allay the same anxieties, torments, and disturbances to which the so-called religions offered answers . . . Capitalism is a religion of pure cult, without dogma.'

Walter Benjamin, 'Capitalism as Religion', in *Selected Writings: Volume 1 1913–1926*, ed. Marcus Bullock and Michael W. Jennings, Belnap Press, 1996, pp. 288–9.

alluding to, such moves represent little more than a silent takeover of religion. Marketing 'the spiritual' allows companies and their consumers to pay lip-service to the 'exotic', rich and historically significant religions of the world at the same time as distancing themselves from any engagement with the worldviews and forms of life that they represent. Religion is rebranded as 'spirituality' in order to support the ideology of capitalism.

A TYPOLOGY OF SPIRITUALITIES IN RELATION TO CAPITALISM

When trying to understand the nature of what we are calling capitalist spirituality, it is necessary to make a number of distinctions in order to appreciate the various relations that exist between contemporary forms of spirituality and capitalism. Although we are not claiming that spirituality should (or indeed could) be separated from economic questions, we do believe that it *should not be fundamentally shaped* by an economic ideology. We wish to challenge the way in which the concept of spirituality is being utilised to 'smooth out' resistance to the growing power of corporate capitalism and consumerism as the defining ideology of our time. We do this not out of some misguided belief that traditional religious institutions and systems have been free from authoritarian and oppressive strictures of their own, but rather out of a concern that cultural diversity is being eroded by the incessant march of a single worldview – an economically driven globalisation – driven by a triumphalist and corporate-oriented form of capitalism.

The Spectrum of Spirituality – Capitalism Relations:
The Different Types

For the purposes of our analysis, one can make a distinction between four degrees of relative accommodation to the ideology of capitalism:

Revolutionary or Anti-Capitalist Spiritualities: such movements reject the capitalist ideology of neoliberalism (life determined by market forces alone) and the pursuit of profit as a goal that can be combined with a recognition of a spiritual, religious or ethical dimension to life. Many of these groups have emerged from within specific religious traditions. They ground their spiritual approaches in a 'this-worldly' commitment to social justice and appeal to a wide range of ancient traditions and movements such as the social critiques of the early Israelite prophets, the Christian Social Gospel movement, Islamic notions of a just economy and universal brotherhood, Buddhist notions of enlightened re-engagement with the world for the sake of alleviating the suffering of others, the radical egalitarian strands of bhakti and Sufi movements in India, etc. Examples of movements and trends that build upon such historical precedents include the various philosophies and theologies of liberation among subaltern groups across the 'Two-Thirds World', socially engaged Buddhism, the deep ecology movement, etc.

Business-Ethics/Reformist Spiritualities: such movements accept the pursuit of profit as a legitimate goal and therefore do not reject the capitalist system in its entirety, but believe in restraining the market in terms of fundamental ethical principles deriving from a particular religious or spiritual perspective on life. There is a long tradition of religious reform of business activities, as found, for instance, in the various religious co-operative movements and the Quaker tradition of ethically oriented business enterprises, as put forward by such authors as Georgeanne Lamont in *The Spirited Business* (see Chapter Four). These forms of spirituality, like Tom Beaudoin's Catholic social ethics and his idea of 'economic spirituality' in his work *Consuming Faith*, seek to find ways of synthesising traditional 'religious' understanding with the values of business and consumer culture. Such approaches accept, with some ethical modification, the status quo of the market and business world, and do not seek to question the underlying basis of its ideology. The emphasis is upon the integration of ethical values into the dominant culture, rather than a radical exploration of how the ethical demands of the religious tradition might require a substantial re-evaluation of the economic system. The ideology of neoliberalism is never placed under radical scrutiny in these forms of spirituality which therefore, in many respects, provide indirect support for a consumerist culture. Such forms, therefore, can easily venture towards and hold aspects of both consumerist and capitalist spirituality, as seen in Tom Beaudoin's work *Consuming Faith* (2003: 106–7):

There is an authentic spiritual impulse at the heart of our branding economy . . . We live out our relation to our ultimate meaning through what and how we buy. Let the integration of faith and economy be the mark of the true spiritual seeker today, a consuming faith.

Individualist/Consumerist Spiritualities: this trend represents an aspect of what is sometimes called 'Prosperity Religion' (for instance US tele-evangelism), but in a modern de-traditionalised setting. The linkage between religious practices and the profit motive are as old as history itself, but 'prosperity religions' is a term generally used by scholars of religion to refer to movements that emerged in the nineteenth century and developed in response to the Industrial Revolution and the rise of modern capitalism. They have tended to be modernist in orientation and are complicitous with the capitalist system at the same time as maintaining strong links to tradition, scripture and religious specificity. As Woodhead and Heelas (2000: 174) note,

> Prosperity religion, of course, is bound up with what would appear to be an ever-more significant feature of modern times: the growth of consumer culture and the associated 'ethicality' – if that is the right term – of people intent on satisfying their consumeristically driven desires. It could well be the case that prosperity religion is (characteristically) about the sacralisation of utilitarian individualism.

What we are here calling 'individualist or consumerist spirituality' relates to a late twentieth-century development within the broader historical phenomenon of 'prosperity religions'. It refers to those who embrace capitalism, consumerism and individualism and interpret their religious or spiritual worldview in terms of these ideologies. Whereas the nineteenth century prosperity religions were generally modernist in origin, the consumerist spiritualities emerged in the late 1960s and are generally 'postmodern' in orientation, with an emphasis upon eclecticism, individualist experimentation and a 'pick and mix' approach to religious traditions. There is much within the 'New Age' and 'Personal Development/Self-Help' movement that exemplifies this trend. Specific examples include Stephen Russell (The

Barefoot Doctor), Sharon Janis (author of *Spirituality for Dummies*) and Maslovian psychology (see Chapters Two and Three for a discussion of these examples).

Capitalist Spiritualities: the subordination and exploitation of religious themes and motifs to promote an individualist and/or corporate-oriented pursuit of profit for its own sake. Capitalist spiritualities are emerging in response to the rise of global finance capitalism. Like the individualist or consumerist spiritualities upon which they have fed, they are 'postmodern' in the sense that, grounded in an information age and the transfer of electronic data across national boundaries, they tend to disavow explicit association with traditional religions, promoting instead a highly eclectic, disengaged and detraditionalised spirituality. This conforms to emerging social trends and the contemporary social Zeitgeist of late capitalist societies. Such trends, however, manifest an uncritical assimilation of business values into their rationale. In many cases, what characterises such trends is a subtle shift beyond an exclusive emphasis upon the individual self and towards a concern with making the individual employee/consumer function as effectively as possible for the benefit of corporate organisations and the 'global economy'.

Traditional religious appeals to the importance of 'community' and social connectedness are here 'rebranded' in terms of the desirability of working for the corporate community or buying more of this or that product. Such a

> 'When the inner self connects to one's work, work and the inner self seem to know no limits.'
>
> Elmer H. Burack, 'Spirituality in the Workplace', *Journal of Organizational Change Management* 12(4), 1999: 284.

move allows advocates of capitalist spirituality to use the traditional language of 'belonging' but this time orient it towards the need for employees to align themselves with the corporate mission statements of their employers, or to reinforce the ideology of consumerism. Examples of this trend include Deepak Chopra, Osho Rajneesh and a variety of authors such as Jesper Kunde ('Corporate Religion'), Carayol and Firth ('Corporate Voodoo') and John Grant ('The New Marketing Manifesto'). See Chapter Four for a discussion of these examples. Some movements maintain an affiliation to a specific religious tradition while expounding a corporatist ethic (such as the Catholic movement Opus Dei and some forms of Neo-Pentecostalism). For a fairly comprehensive list of the literature in this genre to the mid–1990s see Heelas (1996: 66–7).

We offer the above interpretive grid as an alternative to the typology offered by Roy Wallis (1984), which classifies new religious movements in terms of their *world-affirming, world-denying* or *world-accommodating* orientation. Wallis's approach is built upon older (Weberian) classifications of religious attitudes towards the world ('this-worldly' vs. 'other-worldly') and remains useful at a certain level of analysis. However, the typology naively assumes unanimity about what 'the real world' is like (to which each group is said to have a particular orientation), yet this is precisely one of the major points of contention between different traditions and worldviews. Moreover, for the purposes of our current discussion, Wallis's typology is insufficiently focused on attitudes towards capitalism and consumerism to pick out the trends that we wish to explore.

Using our fourth category as our point of orientation, one can classify contemporary forms of spirituality according to the various degrees of accommodation or resistance they exhibit to the following features of what we are calling capitalist spirituality:

1 *Atomisation*: the individualisation of responsibility with no consideration of society.
2 *Self-interest*: an ethic of self-interest that sees profit as the primary motivation for human action.
3 *Corporatism*: placing corporate (not community) success above the welfare and job security of employees.
4 *Utilitarianism*: treating others as means rather than ends (e.g. seeing humans as consumers to be persuaded, other businesses as competitors to be overcome, or employees as resources to be used).
5 *Consumerism*: the promotion of unrestrained desire-fulfilment as the key to happiness.
6 *Quietism*: tacit or overt acceptance of the inevitability of social injustice rather than a wish to overcome it.

7   *Political Myopia*: a claim to political neutrality – the refusal to see the political dimensions of 'spirituality'.

8   *Thought-control/Accommodationism*: use of psycho-physical techniques, described in terms of 'personal development', that seek to pacify feelings of anxiety and disquiet at the individual level rather than seeking to challenge the social, political and economic inequalities that cause such distress.

This list is far from exhaustive, but we hope that it gives the reader a sense of the particular orientation that is associated with capitalist spiritualities. In terms of our fourfold typology, one can read examples of contemporary spirituality in terms of the degree to which they demonstrate conformity or resistance to the above eight characteristics. It is important to appreciate, however, that the typology that we have outlined is an analytic abstraction for the purposes of classification. It should not be read as referring to fixed types, but rather as four points on a dynamic cultural continuum. There may also be some movement along the spectrum of possibilities in the case of specific movements and individuals at different times. No person or movement, for instance, can claim to be free from all of the eight features highlighted above as characteristic of capitalist spirituality. Rather, it is a question of where one can be placed on the spectrum at any given time in terms of one's complicity with such trends. We are not claiming, for instance, to be able to step outside the influence of consumerism and inhabit some 'pure' realm of ethical or spiritual practice.

> We should be done once and for all with the search for an outside, a standpoint that imagines a purity for our politics. It is better both theoretically and practically to enter the terrain of Empire and confront its homogenizing and heterogenizing flows in all their complexity, grounding our analysis in the power of the global multitude.
>
> (Negri and Hardt, 2000: 46)

One of the central concerns of this book is the way that the market-driven economy of corporate capitalism has embraced the concept of 'spirituality'. This cultural ordering of spirituality in the business world exploits the transformative power of traditional 'spiritual' disciplines by reorienting their fundamental goals. Instead of the more traditional emphasis upon self-sacrifice, the disciplining of desire and a recognition of community, we find productivity, work-efficiency and the accumulation of profit put forward as the new goals. In this context, spirituality becomes a way of developing incentives that are conducive to the corporate objectives of the employer. The 'spiritual' becomes instrumental to the market rather than oriented towards a wider social and ethical framework, and its primary function becomes the perpetuation of the consumerist status quo rather than a critical reflection upon it.

What is required is an application of the secularist critique developed by thinkers such as Marx and Nietzsche to the emergence of a capitalist spirituality that is claimed to be non-dogmatic, non-institutional and consumer-oriented. The secularist critique of religion, most famously represented by Marx's claim that religion is the opiate of the masses, now urgently needs to be applied to the ideological institutions and practices of corporate capitalism itself. There is a new set of institutions preaching the gospel of no alternatives and these are the 'Unholy Trinity' of the International Monetary Fund (IMF), the World Bank and the World Trade Organisation (WTO). The religious quality of contemporary capitalism is captured well by former Labour MP Tony Benn:

> Religions have an extraordinary capacity to develop into control mechanisms . . . If I look at the world today it seems to me that the most powerful religion of all – much more powerful than Christianity, Judaism, Islam and so on – is the people who worship money. That is really [the] most powerful religion. And the banks are bigger than the cathedrals, the headquarters of the multinational companies are bigger than the mosques or the synagogues. Every hour on the news we have business news – every hour – it's a sort of hymn to capitalism.
>
> (Benn, 2002)

God is dead, but has been resurrected as 'Capital'. Shopping malls have become the new altars for worshipping the God of money, and consumerism is the new esoteric knowledge (disguised as 'New Age' spirituality).

> We use symbols belonging to a genuinely religious tradition and transform them into formulas serving the purpose of alienated man. Religion has become an empty shell; it has been transformed into a self-help device for increasing one's own powers for success. God becomes a partner in business.
>
> (Fromm, 2004: 73)

Ironically, one way to respond and extend the scope of Marx's initial criticism is to draw upon the traditions of ethical reflection and social justice that are found within the religious traditions themselves. Unfortunately, as Harvard theologian Harvey Cox (2003: 25) points out,

> For the most part . . . religions have addressed economic disparity with alms and charity. They have not – with some important exceptions – confronted the structural sources of inequality. It now appears that those exceptions, like Islamic notions of a righteous economy, the medieval Christian doctrine of the just price, the Social Gospel movement, and liberation theology, need to be brought from the past and from theology's edges into the center of reflection on the ethical responsibilities of a global civilization.

In writing this book we hope to broaden the conversation about the role of religions in modern society. We are certainly not advocating an uncritical return to tradition, but rather wishing to extend the scope of the 'hermeneutics of suspicion' (Marx, Freud, Nietzsche) to so-called secular ideologies and regimes of thought-control in a contemporary context. In this respect we are seeking to articulate a position that speaks to two groups within society – the secularists/ atheists with their wholesale rejection of the religious as oppressive and dogmatic on the one hand, and the religious traditionalists and conservatives who promote the sense of community and ethical virtues of traditional religion, but are unwilling to challenge the conservative and oppressive aspects of religious traditions, on the other. The situation is much more complicated than the ideological positioning of either of these groups suggests.

The 'brilliance' of the capitalist move is found in the way in which it builds upon older colonial legacies and yet manages to portray itself as 'inevitable' and not a form of colonialism at all. The medieval Christians of Europe sought 'to convert the heathen' to the true faith. This, alongside the profit-motive of course, became a key rationale for the colonisation of Asia, Africa and the Americas. In the eighteenth and nineteenth centuries the rise of Enlightenment humanism transformed this into the goal of bringing enlightenment and civilisation to 'the savage'. Meanwhile, Europe flourished with Britain leading the way with an Industrial Revolution premised upon the cheap labour and plundered resources from its Empire in the East. In our contemporary context, the new rationale for colonialism is the conversion of entire communities and societies into individualised 'consumers' and compliant workers. With the rise of neoliberalism in the late twentieth century, the primary ideological rationale for maintaining domination has become the mythology of 'the free market' and the spread of democracy. This rhetoric hides the reliance of the capitalist enterprise upon these older colonial legacies.

In a context where brands and images are becoming more important than the products themselves, 'spirituality' has become the new currency in the task of winning human minds and hearts. Corporate business interests are served by utilising the 'cultural capital' of the religious traditions – building upon their authority base and, in the case of Asian religions, cashing in on their 'exotic image' at the same time as distancing themselves from the traditions. Ancient cultural traditions and systems of thought become commodities like everything else in this brave new world. Our rich and disparate pasts are now up for sale.

OUTLINE OF THE BOOK

In Chapter One we highlight the shifting meanings of 'the spiritual' throughout history. As a result, we should not expect to be able to use terms such as 'spirituality' as if they have some fixed or definitive meaning free from contestation and debate. Although the term 'spirituality' developed from earlier Greek and Latin roots, there are significant dimensions to these earlier uses that are lost once one defines the spiritual in narrowly privatised terms. While previous studies have plotted this genealogy of the term, we seek to show how the concept has been shaped in the modern period by an initial process of individualisation (linked to the privatisation of religion in modern liberal democracies) and then, more recently, by a second form of privatisation, namely corporatisation. Finally, we attempt to show how the contemporary idea of 'spirituality' operates in the context of the rise of neoliberalism as a dominant discourse within society and examine its vagueness and ambiguity, its relation to notions of transcendence and finally its corporate branding. This brief history of the term is then examined in greater detail in the subsequent chapters and the political nature of capitalist spirituality unfolded through its various transformations.

In Chapters Two and Three we explore in detail two major formations of the spiritual from the mid-twentieth century: the impact of psychology upon religion and the development of the modern notion of 'spirituality', and the New Age privatisation of Asian wisdom traditions as forms of 'eastern spirituality'. These processes influenced the shape of western religious thinking and practice in the first half of the twentieth century but, as we shall see, it was not until the second half of the twentieth century that 'spirituality' came to signify a de-institutionalised and privatised religion as it does today.

Chapter Two examines the influence of psychology on the idea of spirituality. We argue that the discourse and institutions of psychology have played a major part in maintaining control in late capitalist societies in the West by creating a privatised and individualised conception of reality. Modern government requires a social mechanism to control populations, and psychology functions, in part, as the underlying philosophy of what it is to be a human for a capitalist system of social organisation. By examining the history of psychology we show how different psychologists have translated 'the religious' into an individualised realm in support of capitalism. The overriding cultural effect of the ideology of psychology is that it masks the social dimension of human existence and creates social isolation.

The process of turning religion into a psychological reality is shown in the contemporary popularity of the idea of 'private spirituality,' which emerges as a product of capitalist psychology. Psychology controls individual consumers by giving them the illusion of unrestrained freedom. It offers the psychological product of 'spirituality' as an apparent cure for the isolation created by a materialistic, competitive and individualised social system. Paradoxically, such notions of spirituality only reinforce social isolation because they tend to be construed in terms of a privatised model of human reality. The psychological turn provided the intellectual platform for the corporate takeover of religion by facilitating the incorporation of religious traditions into the capitalist worldview.

In Chapter Three, we examine some of the Asian 'wisdom' traditions that are so frequently appealed to in contemporary literature on 'spirituality'. Each tradition discussed represents only a small sample of the Buddhist, Hindu and Taoist traditions as a whole, but to consider them all would be impossible in a short work such as this. This selectivity, however, is premised upon a consideration of what is left out in most New Age accounts of these traditions. We hope to establish that there is a great deal within the philosophical ideals and contemplative techniques of these three Asian traditions that offers a challenge, both ideologically and at the level of practice, to the values of a consumerist society. This is not of course in the modern sense of offering an explicit socio-political critique of capitalism (as in the case of, say, Marxism), but rather in each tradition's attempt to counter the human addiction to our (individual, ego-driven) selves as the centre of the universe. From this standpoint we are then in a position to contrast the orientation of such traditional 'Asian wisdom traditions' with the commodified forms in which they are found in the capitalist spirituality and popular New Age markets.

At a cultural level, the shift in interest from 'traditional religion' to 'private spirituality' has overwhelmingly been presented to us as consumer-oriented, that is as reflecting the concerns of the modern, 'liberated' individual to free themselves from the traditional constraints of religion, dogma and ecclesiastical forms of thought-control. This triumphalist celebration of modernity as 'enlightened' and 'liberating' for the individual, however, is not always what it seems. Thus, as we hope to demonstrate in Chapter Four, with the deregulation of the markets in the 1980s and the fall of the Berlin Wall we are seeing the rise of a new phenomenon that builds upon the 1960s and 1970s 'consumerist' approach to religion. This is the emergence of capitalist spirituality, and it amounts to a *corporate-led* takeover of the cultural space carved out in popular culture by terms such as 'spirituality' and 'religion'.

The argument of this book then is that the term 'spirituality' is in the process of being appropriated by business culture to serve the interests of corporate capitalism and worship at the altar of neoliberal ideology. It reflects the takeover of 'the religions' by big business and has resulted in the utilisation of the wholesome and life-affirming connotations of the term 'spirituality' as a means of promoting a market-oriented value system. One can choose to see this in broadly conspiratorial tones as an attempted takeover bid by the leaders of the new world order of global capitalism, but, in our view, it is better understood as a loose network of business-oriented entrepreneurs exploiting a widespread cultural trend that is already in motion. Whatever one's interpretation, what we are seeing is a wholesale infiltration by the sensibilities, language and agenda of corporate business, of the cultural spheres traditionally inhabited by the religions.

This cultural shift in meanings is, of course, not going on uncontested. There are many movements, trends, discourses and individuals that utilise the contemporary language of 'spirituality' but that would reject the individualist and corporatist interpretations increasingly associated with the term once it is made apparent to them. There are others perhaps who are uneasy about terms such as 'spirituality' and the kind of 'vague do-good-ism' that it seems to convey, who would nevertheless be critical of the corporate takeover of religion that it often represents. Finally, there may be those who do not consider themselves to be 'religious' or 'spiritual' in any sense of the term but who would wish to challenge the corporate takeover on social and political grounds. In writing this book we hope to offer something of a wake-up call to such different constituencies and others interested in the link between 'the politics of spirituality' and questions of social justice. As Philip Goodchild (2002: 248) argues,

> The spheres of piety, liberty and right, the provinces of the institutions of religion, government and the judiciary respectively, have been increasingly appropriated by finance capital itself. Religions adapt to make themselves more appealing in a competitive market.

To conclude, the manner in which the corporate takeover of religion is taking place follows a two-stage process. First, since the Enlightenment and the birth of modern political liberalism, we have seen the privatisation of religion. This combined with the emergence of a modern capitalist system has allowed the contemporary notion of consumer-oriented and individualised spiritualities to emerge. Second, we are now seeing the corporatisation of spirituality, that is the tailoring of those individualised spiritualities to fit the needs of corporate business culture in its demand for an efficient, productive and *pacified* workforce. It is these processes that are bringing about the silent takeover of religion, and in this book we seek to challenge this takeover by rethinking the ethical and social dimensions of tradition. There is potentially more to what is being presented to us as 'spirituality' than the ideologies of individualism, corporatism and social conformism.

One

'Spirituality' has no universal meaning and has always reflected political interests.

'When I use a word,' Humpty Dumpty said in rather a scornful tone, 'it means just what I choose it to mean – neither more nor less.'

'The question is,' said Alice, 'whether you *can* make words mean so many different things.'

'The question is,' said Humpty Dumpty, 'which is to be master – that's all.'
Lewis Carroll, *Through the Looking Glass (and What Alice Found There)*

There are perhaps few words in the modern English language as vague and woolly as the notion of 'spirituality'. In a consumer society it can mean anything you want, as long as it sells. The language of spirituality functions in a particular way in order to carry out certain tasks in the cultural landscape, it serves a particular function even in its apparent vagueness of meaning. It carries a vast array of emotions and connotations that in most cases can only be identified by understanding something of the history of the term and also by exploring the specific context of its use. Indeed, the word 'spirituality' is used in so many contexts that it is often difficult to know precisely what people mean by the term. In trying to examine the idea of spirituality it is important to understand its 'use' rather than its 'meaning', or, to recall Foucault, we must consider the relations of power the word sets up rather than what it means. Spirituality functions in different ways at different times and reflects a specific ordering of social relations. It is futile to try to appeal to some reputed 'authentic meaning' of such terms since, as socially constructed ideas, they are always subject to a variety of contested meanings. Nevertheless, the very explosion of the word in contemporary society reflects an increasing co-opting by certain groups within society and a specific order of investments in the social, political and religious world. What is clear is that one reason why the term 'spirituality' functions so well in the market space of business and professional efficiency is precisely because it is a vague signifier that is able to carry multiple meanings without any precision. The very ambiguity of the term means that it can operate across different social and interest groups and in capitalist terms, function to establish a market niche.

In this chapter we wish to raise a series of questions about the idea of 'spirituality' in order to reflect upon current usages of the term and to unravel some of their wider social implications.

> 'Spirituality. It has become a kind of buzz-word of the age.'
>
> Mick Brown, *The Spiritual Tourist*, Bloomsbury, 1998, p. 1.

In reflecting briefly upon the history of the term, we are seeking to contest the way that the idea of 'spirituality' is increasingly being employed in the business world and wider consumerist society as a form of social control. We hope that such analysis will help bring some wider critical perspectives to the discussion and prove useful in exploring alternative models of spirituality from those increasingly gaining currency in a world of triumphalist global capitalism.

One of the most intriguing features of the burgeoning literature on spirituality is the way that authors go to extraordinary levels to define the term and yet face complete exasperation in trying to pin down a definitive meaning (see, for example, Fukuyama and Sevig, 1999; Wright, 2000). Accepting defeat, writers normally employ a general meaning, or a working definition, which enables them to corner a fanciful market space drifting on the vague etymologies of the word. Out of breath, such authors usually resort to differentiating 'spirituality' from 'religion' – an even more complex and vague signifier – appealing to the institutional and tradition-specific 'baggage' that the term 'spiritual' manages to avoid (see Chapter Two).

> To be religious conveys an institutional connotation, prescribed rituals, and established ways of believing; to be spiritual is more personal and

experiential, and has to do with the deepest motivations of life for meaning and wholeness. The first is 'official' religion, standardised, and handed down by religious authorities; the second is 'unoffical', highly individualistic, religion 'à la carte' as Reginald Bibby puts it.

(Roof and Gesch, 1995: 72)

Writers sometimes seek to compartmentalise different spheres of life, incorporating a 'spiritual dimension' that is said to overlap with each area, including body, mind, intellect, emotion and society. In this way, 'the spiritual' is demarcated as a specific dimension of human life, but is also said to refer to all dimensions of human life. Such approaches serve only to reinforce the imprecision of the term and the desire to carve out a market space from within the fabric of life itself. Spirituality becomes both a sub-set of 'everything in life' and 'everything in life'. And so the whirly-gig of meanings arrives at a 'Humpty-Dumpty' word meaning anything that you want it to.

The word 'spiritual' might once have meant simply 'relationship to God' but now it is a Humpty Dumpty word that means whatever the speaker wants it to mean. Thus, whenever someone uses the word 'spiritual' to me I have to ask, 'What do you mean by "spiritual"?'

(Rowe, 2001: 41)

But why, if the term is so vague and ambiguous, is it proving so popular? The reason is that the term spirituality has now become the 'brand-label' for the search for meaning, values, transcendence, hope and connectedness in 'advanced capitalist' societies. The notion operates by compartmentalising questions of human values into an identifiable market space. How then do we begin to find our way out of this maze? It is first necessary to provide a specific genealogy of the term.

HISTORICAL FOUNDATIONS OF THE MODERN TERM 'SPIRITUALITY'

The English and French terms 'spirituality' and 'spiritualité' only emerged in the early modern period and, as one would expect, in response to a constellation of concerns, issues and cultural changes that characterised the time. This, in itself, should be enough to make us wary of those who would use such terms in an uncritical manner, as if they referred to an easily identifiable phenomenon occurring in earlier periods of history and across different cultures. We are not arguing for a return to some reputedly original meaning. Rather, we wish to examine some of the implications of contemporary applications of the term and what interests such uses serve in relation to the political and economic structures of capitalism. Those who make an explicit appeal to etymology and the so-called 'original meaning' of terms are often concerned with masking their own political intentions through an appeal to 'authenticity'. Such approaches are guilty of 'the genetic fallacy', that is the mistaken belief that 'the original meaning' (however one might determine that) is the definitive or true meaning of a term. We explicitly reject such ahistorical approaches because of their failure to appreciate the socially constructed nature of ideas. Truth, as Nietzsche so poetically put it, is a 'mobile army of metaphors'. In any case, why privilege *original* meanings? Language and culture evolve throughout history and terms take on a variety of semantic registers in accordance with the changing social, cultural and political contexts in which they operate. It would be a mistake then to appeal to some 'authentic' meaning for the term 'spirituality', as if such concepts were not embedded in a rich and contested history of usage that shifts according to changing conditions and social agendas. Nevertheless, examination of the genealogy of terms such as 'spirituality' remains an important task in identifying how such concepts have been used and what connotations they bring forward as 'traces' from earlier epochs. Such attention to genealogy allows us to see the effects of power operating in the construction of ideas, in this case the idea of spirituality.

In his 1983 article 'Toward Defining Spirituality', Walter Principe provides a useful overview of the history of the term. Principe's work however is limited by the date in which it was published and so necessarily ignores some of the more important developments in the business 'incorporation' of the word and its post-1980s market explosion (the concern of this book).

The card catalogue of my university's library under the heading
'spirituality' shows that from the 1950s on the term 'spirituality' began
to be and increasingly became a more popular word than terms such
as 'spiritual teaching', 'spiritual life', 'devout life', 'interior life' or 'piety'
that had been used earlier.

(Principe, 1983: 128)

Principe also attempts to work towards a stable definition derived
from the Christian heritage of the term and does not explore the
influence of Asian figures and traditions in the development of
contemporary notions of 'the mystic and spiritual East'.

Although the modern term 'spirituality' only emerged in European
culture in the seventeenth century, it carries with it a number of
connotations and associations from earlier historical periods. The
modern English term 'spirituality' comes from the Latin *spiritualitas*
(itself from the noun *spiritus* – 'the breath of life'). According to
Principe's analysis, we can identify four main phases in the significance of the term. First, there is the *early biblical usage*, referring to the
moral sense of life. In the Greek this is *pneuma*, life in the Spirit of God, as
opposed to the 'carnal life' (Latin *caro*) or life of the 'flesh' (Greek *sarx*).
This should not be seen as the later dualism between body and spirit
that we find in the Greek philosophers and early Christian writers
of Late Antiquity, but refers instead to a moral order or way of
life involving the *disciplining of the flesh* – that is the controlling of
unrestrained desires. This element of the term continues to resonate
in later uses where an emphasis is sometimes placed upon the practice
of a rigorous disciplinary regime (often ascetic in nature) in order
to overcome selfish desires and 'the pleasures of the flesh'. In the
New Testament letters of Paul we find this call to moral life in the
spirit (Galatians 3.3; 5.13, 16–25; Corinthians 3.1–3; Romans 7–8).
Both the Greek *pneuma* and the earlier Hebrew *ruah* find their root in
notions of 'air' and 'breath'. In many ways, this very general sense of
something which gives life or 'animates' is still carried forward today.

A second use of the term also emerges under Christian Hellenistic
influence, and this is one that polarises 'spirit' and 'matter'. The
various Gnostic movements of the early Christian period often dis-

tinguished the realm of 'the spiritual' (in Greek *pneumatikos*) from the world of matter (*hylé*). Origen, the third-century Christian writer, made an explicit distinction between three levels of biblical inter-pretation related to the Pauline distinction between body, soul and spirit. First, there is the material level (the literal meaning of biblical words). Second, we have the level which speaks to the specific con-ditions and life of the soul (Greek *psyche*) of the Christian devotee. Third, there is the level of allegorical meaning – where biblical teachings are said to convey universal truths and are not to be read as merely referring to specific historical events. This third level of meaning for Origen corresponded to the 'spiritual' (Greek *pneumatikos*) meaning of the biblical message and is timeless in its significance. While this ancient distinction is not the same as our modern distinction between 'literal' and 'allegorical', we can see the continuing resonance of this kind of theme when we find appeals made to the 'spirit' rather than the 'letter' of a document or law. In our contemporary era, how-ever, the earlier Christian distinction between 'body–soul–spirit' has become recast in terms of the modern notion of an interior, psycho-logical self. The 'spiritual meaning' that once referred to the timeless realm of the Holy Spirit becomes instead 'the inner personal meaning' for the individual, and 'spirituality' becomes associated with an 'inner personal self' (or what approximates in some sense to Origen's second level of the psyche). Spirit and soul become confuted and the 'trans-personal' dimension of the former is lost. Indeed in many ways it is this older Christian structure of 'body–soul–spirit' that has now become secularised and translated into the idea of a specific genre of literature that can be classified for the sake of a publishing market as 'mind, body, and spirit'.

Throughout late Antiquity we find evidence of a distinction between 'spirit', and 'matter', influenced by various strands of Neopla-tonic and Hermetic thought, but mostly through the medium of Greek terms like *pneuma* and *hylé*. According to Principe, specific use of the Latin term from which we derive the English and French terms 'spirituality' and 'spiritualité' can be found in a ninth-century usage that opposes *spiritualitas* to *corporalitas* or *materialitas* in the work of Candidus, thought to be a monk of Fulda. Such dualistic trends were

also promoted within European culture by 'heretical' groups such as
the Albigensian Cathars and the Manichean traditions. What we see
here is a clear shift from the earlier Pauline moral sense and multi-
levelled theories of biblical interpretation to a clear philosophical
dualism between spirit and matter. A key figure in promoting such
a use of the term *spiritualitas*, according to Principe, was the twelfth-
century writer Gilbert of Poitiers.

A third usage of the term relates to ecclesiastical jurisdiction and
property in the medieval period. Here a distinction was made with
regard to persons and property by designating them as either spiritual
or temporal. This allowed a distinction to be drawn between the
'Lords spiritual' and the 'Lords temporal', that is between property
owned by the Church and that owned by the king. This usage, of
course, builds upon much older biblical notions such as 'render unto
Caesar' (Matthew 22.21; Mark 12.17; Luke 20.25) and Origen's distinction between the temporal 'fleshy' meaning of biblical statements
and their timeless 'spiritual' meaning. Mention should also be made of
Ignatius of Loyola (1491–1556), founder of the Company of Jesus,
later known as the Society of Jesus, or the Jesuits. Ignatius wrote a
book in Spanish ('the Autograph') in 1522 that later came to be
known as *The Spiritual Exercises of Ignatius of Loyola*. The work essentially
consists of guidance for those on retreat. It consists mainly of notes
concerning interior movements within the soul that Ignatius noticed
within himself after a conversion experience while recovering from a
leg-wound inflicted during battle in 1521. Ignatius provides thoughts
on how to live a disciplined and contemplative life of the Spirit. He
explicitly distinguishes his 'spiritual exercises', which relate to interiorised contemplative practices of the soul in relation to God, from
everyday bodily exercises.

> [B]y this name of Spiritual Exercises is meant every way of examining
> one's conscience, of meditating, of contemplating, of praying vocally
> and mentally, and of performing other spiritual actions, as will be said
> later. For as strolling, walking and running are bodily exercises, so
> every way of preparing and disposing the soul to rid itself of all the
> disordered tendencies, and, after it is rid, to seek and find the Divine

Will as to the management of one's life for the salvation of the soul, is called a Spiritual Exercise.

(The first annotation from *The Spiritual Exercises* of St Ignatius of Loyola)

THE EMERGENCE OF THE MODERN TERM 'SPIRITUALITY'

Examples such as Ignatius of Loyola provide important precursors of the fourth meaning highlighted by Principe, which he locates as emerging first in seventeenth-century France with the coining of the modern French word *spiritualité*. Here the term signified the devout or contemplative life in general and it is from this word that we derive the modern English term 'spirituality'. By this time, the Protestant Reformation, with its emphasis upon the individual's unmediated relationship to God and the importance of an interior faith, had created a climate within European Christianity which allowed the first steps towards the privatisation of religion to occur. By the seventeenth century, influenced by figures such as Madame Guyon (1648–1717), a new sensibility began to emerge which specifically associated *spiritualité* with the interior life of the individual soul.

> Against the dogmatic tyranny of the established churches and their demand for a conformist piety, and against the claims of reason in matters of faith, a new religious conscience emerged in Europe at the end of the seventeenth century. This new spirit understood religion in terms of individual conscience and lived experience for all people, rather than for only a few . . . For subscribers to this new religious spirit, the hierarchical Church ceased to be conceived as a structure allowing a communication between Heaven and Earth, and collective adherence came to be replaced by individual conscience. The idea arose that religion could no longer be identified with a particular confession, whether Catholic or Protestant.
>
> (Bruneau, 1998: 146–7)

Unlike Ignatius's *Exercises*, which involved using the faculties of the mind in order to focus upon the object of meditation, Guyon promoted the practice of *orison* – a silencing of all mental activities and an abandonment of self in order to experience the divine within oneself. In so doing, Guyon was drawing explicitly upon a much older tradition of practice that has become known as 'negative theology' or 'apophatic mysticism' within the Christian tradition. Although drawing upon such practices, in Madame Guyon's writings spiritualité came to refer specifically to a kind of interiorised knowledge or experience of the divine. It was in 1676, following the death of her husband, that during a reading experience she received what she believed was a deep religious insight. Guyon's writings and advocacy of a pacifying of the individual-will drew criticism from Catholic authorities at the time who criticised her for Quietism – that is the (heretical) belief that contemplation of God leads to a renunciation of all action. Guyon countered this interpretation of her work, arguing that the destruction of self-will that she advocated did not mean a cessation of action as such but rather 'that we should act through the internal agency of grace' (Guyon, *A Short and Very Easy Method of Prayer*, ch. 21). Consequently, the word spiritualité that emerged at this time in relation to figures such as Guyon generally retained pejorative associations with passivity and interiorised self-indulgence, with negative criticism from later figures such as Voltaire, who openly ridicules Madame Guyon as 'a woman of revelations, prophecies and gibberish, who suffocated from interior grace to the point of having to be unlaced' (Voltaire, *Siécle de Louis XIV*, 1847, p. 453, translation in Bruneau, 1998: 192) Similarly, Jonathan Swift satirised Quaker 'spiritual exercises' as 'orgasmus' in his *Discourse Concerning the Mechanical Operation of the Spirit* (1704).

SPIRITUALITY AND THE FIRST PRIVATISATION OF RELIGION

The Romanticist reaction to the rationalist philosophies of the Enlightenment led figures such as the German Protestant theologian Friedrich Schleiermacher (1768–1834) to emphasise the importance of 'feeling' in the religious life. In his 1821 work *The Christian Faith*, Schleiermacher characterised the experience of God as a 'feeling of absolute dependence'. Reflections upon the interior life had always been an important part of the Christian tradition, at least since Augustine's *Confessions* (c.418) and his *De Trinitate* (c.431), but this trend received greater force during the Reformation, with its emphasis upon the relationship of the individual to God. In the nineteenth century, the introspection of the German theological tradition played an important part in the emergence of the discipline of psychology in the 1870s and opened the way for locating 'spirituality' within the individual self (see Chapter Two).

Despite the emergence of the term in the seventeenth century, there was relatively infrequent use of the term *spiritualité* until the late nineteenth and early twentieth centuries. Debates about the nature and value of 'spirituality' in the nineteenth and twentieth centuries continued to reflect a number of broader tensions within European and North American societies at the time: between Romanticism and the Enlightenment, between the truth-claims of traditional religions and those of the emerging sciences, the conflict between allegiance to traditional, institutionalised religions and the new social freedoms that allowed for the exploration of various lifestyle alternatives and options. At the same time, European colonialism had precipitated an unprecedented (if unequal) encounter with various Asian cilivisations. The result was a great deal of popular interest in the exoticism of 'the Orient'.

During this period terms such as 'mysticism' and 'spirituality' provided the conceptual site for these various tensions to express themselves. The popular appeal of 'the spiritual' at this time is a result of the confluence of a number of trends, movements and figures. First, we find the growing popularity of spiritualism and interest in 'the occult', particularly in North America and Britain, complete with oujia boards, *séances* and manifestations of 'ectoplasm' (the mysterious substance that many spirit-mediums were said to vomit when in a trance or possession state). At the same time, inspired by various western orientalist works on the mysteries of the East, European and American audiences became increasingly interested in 'eastern philosophies' and religions, particularly insofar as they seemed to offer an 'exotic' alternative to mainstream Christianity. Figures such as Swami Vivekananda from India, Anagarika Dharmapala from Sri Lanka and Shaku Sôen and his disciple D. T. Suzuki from Japan, came to be seen as modern spokesmen for entire religious traditions. Central to the growing popularity of the notion of 'spirituality' in the late nineteenth and early twentieth century British context was the figure of Vivekananda, follower of the mystical teachings of Ramakrishna, and founder of the Ramakrishna Mission, an organisation aiming to promote the teachings of Advaita (nondualist) Vedanta as the central teaching of Hinduism. Vivekananda built upon prevailing western stereotypes about the technological and material superiority of the West to argue that, while the West was indeed superior in narrowly materialistic terms, it lacked what India had, namely an abundance of spirituality. In so arguing, Vivekananda effectively turned the tables on many western critics of 'backward' India by appealing to prevailing Romantic and orientalist notions of the mystical and exotic East. In so doing, Vivekananda and other figures such as D. T. Suzuki established the basic terms under which the New Age appropriation of Asian wisdom traditions was to proceed in the twentieth century (King, 1999a: ch. 6). 'Eastern spirituality' was born as a concept.

Vivekananda's approach involved exploiting both the association of India with 'the spiritual' and the cultural dichotomy it implied between 'spirituality' and secular philosophies promoting materialism. The link between the burgeoning interest in *spiritualism*, which involved contacting dearly departed spirits through a medium or psychic, and Vivekananda's notion of 'eastern *spirituality*' is not an obvious one. However, the link was made explicitly by Helena Petrovna Blavatsky, one of the founders of the Theosophical Society, in her claim to be in contact with a higher spiritual brotherhood of enlightened masters from the East, from whom she gained her knowledge of theosophical teachings. Given the nature of the competition at the time, Blavatsky spent considerable time countering the claims of the spiritualist movements of her day. Her main argument was that by contacting recently departed personalities mediums served only to prevent the soul from transcending its current embodiment. This held back its creative development in terms of preparing for its next incarnation, but also conflicted with the underlying truth to be realised, according to Blavatsky, namely that

> 'Up India, and conquer the world with your spirituality . . . Ours is a religion of which Buddhism, with all its greatness is a rebel child and of which Christianity is a patchy imitation.'
>
> Swami Vivekananda, *The Complete Works*, 13th edition, vol. 3, 1970, p. 275.

the individual self was an illusion to be overcome by realising our identity with the impersonal cosmic self (*Atman*) of the Hindu *Upanishads*. As Peter van der Veer (2001: 74) notes,

> It is Vivekananda's social reformism, and anticolonial, anti-Christian radicalism that connects him to the spiritualists in Britain. Although the same word – spirituality – was used in English, the unifying language of the empire, it had very different meanings where it stood in relation to Christian traditions in the metropole and to Hindu traditions in the colony. The point here is that these divergences did not stand in the way of a shared antinomian radicalism against the state in Britain and the colonial state in India.

The terms 'spirituality' and 'spiritualism', while associated by many with largely private and 'other-worldly' mystical pursuits, were at the same time associated by others, such as the socialist and theosophist Annie Besant (1847–1933), with social reform, political activism and the pursuit of economic and social justice. In the British context, at least, this partly related to working-class and anti-Establishment trends within these movements. Indeed, as van der Veer (2001: 58) has suggested, 'spiritualism, and Theosophy in particular, played a significant role in the development of radical anticolonial politics both in Britain and India'. The overwhelming trend over time however has been to emphasise the association of 'spirituality' with the interior life of the individual. Such an orientation is clearly not in itself incompatible with a socially engaged perspective, but it becomes so once 'the individual' is conceived as an independent, autonomous and largely self-contained entity within society. Such closure, establishing the impermeable boundaries of the modern, individual self, under-mines an awareness of interdependence and erodes our sense of solidarity with others. The consolidation of this privatising trend is bound up with the emerging cultural force of psychology in the twentieth century and its involvement with the rise of new forms of life linked to the capitalist reorganisation of European and North American societies after World War Two. It was North American psychologists such as William James, Gordon Allport and Abraham Maslow who were to play a key role in this history (see Chapter Two).

Principe suggests that it is only from 1950 that we see an enormous increase in use of the term spirituality in popular culture in the West. This date is perhaps significant because of the post-war economic and political conditions that coincide with the rise of the modern consumerist lifestyle and enable the term to take on new connotations. For example, Alcoholics Anonymous (AA), in part inspired by the work of psychologist Carl Jung, endorsed a 12-Step spiritual path of recovery and promoted belief in a 'higher power' and 'mysticism' in the 1950s and 1960s (Tonigan et al., 1999). This programme has helped thousands of sufferers but it nonetheless reflected a growing psychologisation of human experience (see Chapter Two) that is, and was, part of a wider cultural shift. Ironically, the neglect of the social dimensions of 'spirituality' and 'the self' within mainstream psychological discourse has itself contributed to a new cultural malaise – the loneliness and isolation of contemporary individualism.

Between 1950 and 1980 we find the term 'spirituality' increasingly used to refer to the life and work of particular figures in religious history, such as the 'spirituality' of Ignatius of Loyola, John Calvin or Teilhard de Chardin. This is also extended to refer to religious traditions as a whole, so that we can now talk of the spirituality of Judaism or the spirituality of Japanese Buddhism. The Christian theological usage of the term also expands, with the spirituality of the Mass, the spirituality of the sacraments and the spirituality of mission gaining increasing currency at this time. We also see the production of 'histories of Christian spirituality' and more popular spiritualities for the Church in the USA. This reflects the expansion of ideas about spirituality found in American humanistic psychology, which also drew upon Asian philosophical traditions (see Chapter Two). One striking example noted at the end of Principe's history is the shift in title in 1972 of the *Revue d'ascétique et de mystique* (Journal of Asceticism and Mysticism) to the *Revue d'histoire de la spiritualité* (Journal of the History of Spirituality). This example is important because it reflects the cultural shift from concerns with 'mysticism' to an interest in 'spirituality'. The notion of spirituality overlapped with a discourse of mysticism until the late 1980s, but the notion of mysticism has been increasingly replaced by references to 'the spiritual'. Spirituality flourished as an idea in this context because it found a place within 'secular' markets, whereas 'mysticism' still retained its other-worldly and tradition-based connotations. While both spirituality and mysticism went through the process of psychologisation, the former has emerged as preferable in designating a de-traditionalised and this-worldly phenomenon in western society at the beginning of the twenty-first century. 'Mysticism' still carries with it the connotations of occultism, mystery and association with particular 'world religions'. In that sense the term 'mysticism' has lost much of its earlier appeal precisely because it has remained strongly associated with religion and the supernatural, ideas that have been largely eradicated from the 'this-worldly' and individualistic uses of the term 'spirituality'.

The post-war construction of spirituality carried forward two main aspects that held within them the tensions of post-Enlightenment (eighteenth/nineteenth-century) thinking. The rejection of materialism and institutional forms of (Christian) religion in Romanticism often expressed itself in terms of a preoccupation with Asian 'mystical' traditions and culture. Similarly, the Romanticist celebration of the creative genius of the individual had already claimed to liberate human sentiment from its institutional moorings. With the establishment of psychology as the pre-eminent 'science of the self' in the post-war period, we see an increasingly 'non-religious' understanding of spirituality emerge. This changing climate within modern capitalist societies has led many traditions, including established western ones such as Christianity, to 'de-mythologise', by moving away from the older cosmological and disciplinary language of the past and replacing this with the interiorised and psychologically inflected language of 'spirituality'. The ongoing influence of western orientalist fantasies of the East brought new dimensions to this notion of interiority, something Carl Jung had recognised earlier in the twentieth century.

It seems to be quite true that the East is at the bottom of the spiritual change we are passing through today. Only this East is not a Tibetan monastery full of Mahatmas, but in a sense lies within us. It is from the depths of our own psychic life that new spiritual forms will arise; they will be expressions of psychic forces which may help to subdue the boundless lust for prey of Aryan man.

(Jung, 1984: 250)

THE EMERGENCE OF CAPITALIST SPIRITUALITY: THE SECOND PRIVATISATION OF RELIGION

The interiorisation of spirituality and its location within the bounds of the modern, individual self emerged with the development of psychology in the late nineteenth century. It became popularised, however, in the 1950s and 1960s with the rise of Humanistic Psychology (particularly the work of Maslow), professional counselling and psychedelic culture (see Chapter Two). Having been cast as a private and psychological phenomenon, 'spirituality' has gone through a second major shift in the 1980s. This is the point at which the first privatisation – involving the creation of individual, consumer-oriented spiritualities – begins to overlap with an increasing emphasis upon a second privatisation of religion – that is, the tailoring of spiritual teachings to the demands of the economy and of individual self-expression to business success. This is no better illustrated than by the various self-improvement movements of the 1980s, which, as Baumann (1998: 72) suggests,

> are products and integral parts of the 'counselling boom' – though they are not, like other branches of counselling, meant to serve directly the consumer choices of assumedly fully-fledged consumers, but are aimed rather at the training of '*perfect consumers*'; at developing to the full the capacities which the experience-seeking and sensation-gathering life of the consumer/chooser demands.

Following the deregulation of the markets by Margaret Thatcher and Ronald Reagan and the rise of neoliberalism as the global ideology of our age, cultural forms have themselves become commodities. For the first time in human history, economics has begun to dictate the terms of expression for the rest of the social world. Now, unhinged from the social to an unprecedented degree, the market is able to dictate the cultural and political agenda and take over the processes of socialisation (such as the cultivation and disciplining of individual appetites) that have been traditionally carried out by religious and state institutions.

In this climate, 'spirituality' becomes one of a number of ways of shaping individual sensibilities in terms of a new regime of power, this time dominated by the demands of corporate enterprise and the need for a flexible and compliant workforce. Thus, in the late 1980s and 1990s, public institutions in the UK and USA (and much further afield) carry forward both forms of privatised 'spirituality' into their working practices. In this way, some of the contradictions between individualist or consumer-oriented and corporate-oriented approaches to spirituality are concealed. With the emergence of capitalist spirituality the freedom of the individual to express their inner nature through 'spirituality' becomes subordinated to the demands of corporate business culture and the needs of a flexible and competitive economy. This represents a shift from the earlier phase of 'consumer-led' spiritual enquiry, which emphasised the individual's freedom to choose his or her own pathway in life (the bedrock of modern liberalism), to a 'corporate-led' consumerism that subordinates the interests of the individual to consumerist ideology and the demands of the business world (neoliberalism).

The result is the current explosion of usage of the term 'spirituality' in educational, medical and corporate contexts. For example, the word 'spiritual' appears in UK government revisions of education in the 1988 Education Reform Act with the specification that children should be taught a balanced and broad-based curriculum. Such education should promote 'the spiritual, moral, cultural, mental and physical development of pupils at the school and of society' (HMSO, 1988, p. 1). As a result, spirituality becomes for the first time the subject of national educational planning, with numerous studies and texbooks devoted to the idea and its application and significance for children's minds. In such a climate, 'spirituality' is not only a new form of socialisation but also becomes a new means of thought-control, carried into ever-wider spheres of life for a new generation of innocent consumers. From the 1980s, spirituality infiltrates all domains of public life, including healthcare, education and, most significantly in terms of the current study, the world of business. Indeed, spirituality can be mixed with anything since, as a positive but largely vacuous cultural trope, it manages to imbue any product with a wholesome and life-affirming quality. The proliferation of 'spirituality' and 'personal development' literature since the 1980s also reflects the capitalist takeover and privatisation of human meaning – all the more sinister for the way in which it is celebrated as 'holistic' and 'ethically' virtuous. The economic ideology of neo-liberalism, with its fundamentalist adherence to 'deregulating the market', has entered the public space of religion in its disguised form as 'spirituality'. The result is a proliferation of literature linking spirituality to all aspects of life, with a specific emphasis upon its relevance for the 'helping professions' and business world. Consider the following examples of contemporary Book titles:

Spirituality and Education
Spirituality and Psychotherapy
Spirituality and Medicine
Spirituality and Nursing
Spirituality and Mental Health
Spirituality and Multiculturalism
Spirituality and the Workplace
Spirituality and Business
Spirituality and Management
Spirituality and the Young, Old and Mature
Spirituality and Dying
Spirituality and UFOs

The modern emergence of 'spirituality' reflects the ongoing malleability of the term 'spiritual' and its formation according to changing political circumstances. The early Christian usage of 'spiritual' was a moral-political distinction asserting a new truth and revelation. The use of the term to demarcate land rights by the spiritual designation showed the assertion of territorial rights, and Madame Guyon's courageous claim for an inner authority became a battle against the power of the Church. The use of the term against materialism, against colonial domination, and against religious dogmatism and conformity are all instances where the concept is articulated in the context of important social struggles. The notion of 'the spiritual' then has always been a space of contestation for human values across differing institutional forces, groups and constituencies. There have been, and continue to be, a wide range of activists and social movements that contest the individualisation of the spiritual. This, however, has rarely been informed by any systematic reflection upon the predominance of the 'privatised spirituality' model and the ease with which reference to 'the spiritual' becomes domesticated by an emphasis upon individual interiority. The 'spiritual', nonetheless, remains an active signifier for human experience and shows the power of representation in history and contemporary society.

> 'To begin with, the recent rise of the "spiritual" as a category of popular religious idiom cannot be understood apart from considerations of religious and cultural power.'
>
> Wade Clark Roof, *Spiritual Marketplace*, Princeton University Press, 1999, p. 89.

MULTIPLE MEANINGS: JUMPING DOWN THE NEOLIBERAL RABBIT HOLE

The rabbit-hole went straight on like a tunnel for some way, then dipped suddenly down, so suddenly that Alice had not a moment to think about stopping herself before she found herself falling down what seemed to be a very deep hole . . . Down, down, down. Would the fall *never* come to an end?

Lewis Carroll, *Alice's Adventures in Wonderland*, Heinemann, 1948, pp. 2, 4

In order to appreciate the way 'spirituality' is increasingly being shaped by the agenda of neoliberalism, it is worth examining some of the problems of definition and contemporary application that surround the term. First, its *vagueness and ambiguity* allows it to mask the underlying ideologies that it is used to represent. Second, we shall consider the term's *relation to religion and the idea of transcendence*, and, third, the latest phase in its construction, namely the *corporate rebranding of spirituality*.

(a) Vagueness and Ambiguity

The striking feature of the contemporary usage of the term is the way in which it veers across popularly accepted divisions between 'religious' and 'non-religious' realms of life. Part of the success of the term has been its ability to range from meaning something as simple as 'increased awareness' to more specific references to traditional meditative disciplines and/or religious beliefs. Clive Beck (1986) identifies the wide range of contemporary meanings from insight to love, from mind–body–spirit integration to optimism, from energy, a sense of transcendence to an acceptance of the inevitable, etc. This 'mish-mash' of meanings reflects its operational neutrality for marketing purposes. Similarly, the theologian John Swinton (2001: 25) has plotted the referential spectrum of the term in a modern context with its rather vague emphasis upon meaning, value, transcendence, connection and becoming. William Miller and Carl Thoresen discuss 'spirituality' within and beyond specific religious traditions and, echoing the Maslovian tradition (that we shall discuss in Chapter Two), point towards 'spirituality in Silicon Valley'. This is said to include 'mountain biking at dusk, quiet contemplation of nature, reflection on the direction of one's life, and a feeling of intimate connection with loved ones' (Miller and Thoresen, 1999: 7). These may well be fundamentally valuable experiences. What is it, however, that makes them 'spiritual'? Whose interests does such a classification serve? Examine any of the books in the vast literature defining spirituality and you will find the same problem of a diverse range of experiences being reordered and classified under this new catch-all term.

One striking example of the way in which the vagueness of the term masks an underlying ideology can be seen in some of the early discussions of the use of spirituality in contemporary educational reform in the UK. The British educationalist David Lambourn (1996) highlights the category error in British government documentation (National Curriculum Council) and argues that just as there is no 'God of the gaps' to fill in the spaces where science fails, so there could be no 'spirituality of the gaps' to fill in what cannot be described. School pupils are encouraged to appreciate a 'sense of awe, wonder and mystery' as part of a programme of study. Paradoxically, the very instruction to cultivate such experiences as part of a prescribed national curriculum undermines the likelihood of success. More importantly, he finishes his essay by expressing a suspicion that spirituality 'was being used to smuggle something in which perhaps should be examined more explicitly' (Lambourn 1996: 157). Lambourn offers no suggestions as to what is being smuggled into the minds of British schoolchildren. The wider politic influencing this terminology needs to be examined. In our view this reflects a wider cultural reorientation of life according to a set of values that commodifies human experience and opens up the space for the corporate takeover of all human knowledge and life.

Lambourn was rightly suspicious, for behind the sugary veneer of spirituality lies a subtle form of privatisation, now increasingly linked to the marketisation of all dimensions of human life. It is in fact an important step in the silent takeover of religion. Like Alice in Wonderland who falls down the rabbit hole into another world, spirituality deflects criticism and obscures meaning. Some, enjoying the comfort zone of 'feel-good' spirituality, will resist our attempts to examine the political and economic ideologies it sustains. Failure to examine the neoliberal framing of spirituality in contemporary culture, however, leads to collusion rather than resistance to the desacralisation and commodification of life. The ambiguity and imprecision of the concept of spirituality acts as an effective cover for its ideological application.

(b) Relation to Religion and the Idea of Transcendence

Alongside the ambiguity of the term spirituality is the association of the word with 'transcendence'. Almost all definitions of the modern term make some reference to this idea, but the meaning is often unclear. As Lambourn wryly notes, how are government inspectors to evaluate the implementa-

> 'Experience feelings of transcendence – feelings which may give rise to belief in the existence of a divine being, or the belief that one's inner resources provide the ability to rise above everyday experiences.'
>
> National Curriculum Council, 1993: 2, cited in Lambourn, 1996: 156.

tion of a curriculum that involves cultivating an experience of 'transcendence'? What we see for example in government national curriculum guidance in the UK is a hidden confusion of categories.

The government definition makes a distinction between 'belief in divine beings' and 'personal transformation'. Here, we see the way spirituality crosses different registers of meaning. It is both an ontological transcendence (representing belief in a non-empirical reality) and an immanent (that is internalised) form of personal self-transcendence with no referent beyond the individual. This distinction

> 'What is conspicuously new in today's spirituality is the frequent absence of an explicit transcendent object outside the self.'
>
> David Wulff, Psychology of Religion, 1997, p. 7.

reflects government acknowledgement of the possibility of 'religious' and 'non-religious' forms of spirituality, reflecting its effectiveness in carrying multiple meanings across the secular–religious divide. The business usage of spirituality almost always carries the latter interiorised meaning of 'self-transcendence'. This makes it easier to construct a spirituality that remains firmly located within the individual self rather than oriented towards society.

For example, in her popular book *Spirituality for Dummies* (2000), Sharon Janis provides a typical example of what we have called 'individualist' or 'consumerist spirituality' – that is a reading of 'spirituality' that is principally constructed according to questions of how it meets individual needs and self-interest. For instance, consider the questions Janis asks in the 'Spirituality Check-List' in *Spirituality for Dummies*:

Ten Good Spiritual Questions to Ask Yourself
Who am I?
What is the purpose of my life?
How can my purpose be fulfilled?
What motivates me to do what I do?
What am I searching for?
What keeps me going in my day-to-day life?
What is real?
Why do I care?
Why do I work?
Why do I love?

If Lambourn was concerned about how spirituality and transcendence could be evaluated by government inspectors, turning to Danah Zohar and Ian Marshall's *Spiritual Intelligence: The Ultimate Intelligence* (2001) we can perhaps see the culture of measurement and efficiency entering the spiritual marketplace. According to Zohar and Marshall, alongside IQ (intelligence tests) and EQ (emotional intelligence) we now have SQ (Spiritual Intelligence). Robert Emmons (1999), a psychologist and academic at the University of California at Davis, suggests that there are five core features of 'Spiritual Intelligence'. They are:

1 Capacity for transcendence of immediate material concerns;
2 Ability to experience a heightened state of consciousness;
3 Ability to sanctify everyday activities such as work and relationships;
4 Capacity to utilise spiritual resources to solve problems;
5 Ability to engage in virtuous behaviour (such as forgiveness, gratitude, humility and compassion).

In an attempt to blend science, popular psychology and religion, Zohar and Marshall (2001) perform all of the trademark definitional tricks, separating spirituality from religion while using religious ideas and appealing to the imprecision of meaning in order to link spirituality to the desired area of marketability – in this case popular neuroscience and 'New Age' readings of classical Asian thought. Zohar and Marshall's model is fascinating for the way in which it meanders across immanent and transcendent models of the self. They wish to resist quantification ('spiritual intelligence cannot be quantified', 2001: 276) but nevertheless use the language of assessment and personality types throughout. The authors even claim that it is possible to distinguish between spiritual 'intelligence' and spiritual 'dumbness' and suggest that we can be 'spiritually intelligent about religion' (2001: 292). Spirituality now acts as a register *outside religion* to evaluate the effectiveness of an attitude, question or belief.

> A very religious person may be spiritually dumb; a hard-and-fast atheist may be spiritually intelligent . . . It is certainly not a difference *between* religions, for there are spiritually dumb and spiritually intelligent versions of every religion on the planet. The difference lies in my attitude, in the quality of my questioning and my searching, in the depth and breadth of my beliefs, in the deep source of my beliefs.
>
> (Zohar and Marshall, 2001: 292)

Psychological tests, such as Myers-Briggs Personality Test – using Carl Jung's typology of introversion, extroversion, thinking, feeling, sensation and intuition – have been used to assess spiritual types for some years. This reflects part of the wider privatisation of religion that we will explore in the next chapter, but what also appears in this process of assessment is a marketing mentality. Once spirituality has entered the realm of assessment we are never far from the culture of measurement and productivity. Spirituality is located neatly into a type or an evaluated form and ceases to be a mystery or a complex devotional way of life. It becomes a product and a package. It is, in this sense, no surprise that the psychological theories of both Jung and Maslow have been embraced by the business world. They provide useful ways of marking out efficiency. While Zohar and Marshall are not going this far, and in some of their earlier works, such as *The Quantum Society* (1993), they seek to address the wider social dimensions of the spiritual, the notion of 'spiritual intelligence' reflects the political shift in modern, western culture (and in the domain of religion and spirituality) towards the quantification of human experience and capability and its utilisation in the pursuit of greater worker efficiency, productivity and compliance. This reflects the obsession with measurement and quantification that characterises our age.

> What makes this such a peculiar moment in the history of measurement is that almost every area of public life, qualities like happiness, competence or loyalty are being picked over by hoards of radical accountants and politicians, visionary entrepreneurs and planners – desperately trying to find ways of being more effective in a competitive world.
>
> (Boyle, 2001: xiv)

When employees are encouraged to 'transcend' material discomfort and consider work to be a sacred activity (as in Emmon's five characteristics of the 'spiritually intelligent' person), we are able to see the complicity, whether intentional or not, between these ways of characterising the individual and a corporate capitalist agenda. Why, one wonders, is dissatisfaction with social injustice and a willingness to resist exploitation not seen as a sign of 'spiritual intelligence'? The answer is simple. Such ideas echo a wider cultural ideology of 'excellence' and 'efficiency' that surrounds the classroom, the office and the market. It reflects the ideological links between psychology and capitalism.

(c) The 1990s 'Branding' of Spirituality

The slow process of privatising spirituality in the twentieth century through the influence of 'the psy disciplines' (Rose, 1998) has paved the way for a second privatisation, the corporate takeover of spirituality. In this instance, spirituality is turned into a product or a kind of brand name for the meaning of life (see Chapter Four).

> 'With this wave of brand mania has come a new breed of business, one who will proudly inform you that Brand X is not a product but a way of life, an attitude, a set of values, a look, an idea.'
>
> Naomi Klein, No Logo, Flamingo, 2001, p. 23.

Spirituality is the new 'Brand X' that Naomi Klein identified in her study of corporate business, except that this promise of new life is not attached to a specific product, it remains a merchandising label for all sorts of undefined ideas about the inner-self, wholesomeness and quality of life. The very versatility of the term spirituality is the key to its success. It can mean anything and be attached to any realm of life. Alongside TVs, hi-fi systems, washing machines, IKEA furniture and designer clothes, you can also have your very own spirituality, with or without crystals! In this context consumerism is no longer presented as a challenge to traditional religious sensibilities, because you can now buy it wholesale and ignore the corporate links to poverty and social injustice. As long as you feel good and are able to embrace your own private spiritual world you are assured of a place in the nirvana or heaven of corporate capitalism. You can buy your way to happiness with your very own spirituality, cut off from all the suffering and ills of the world and index-linked to the latest business success. Spirituality has arrived in the corporate marketplace and all that is required is a desire to consume.

Two

'Spirituality' embodies the privatisation of religion in modern, western societies.

M. Scott Peck's *The Road Less Travelled* (1978) is unquestionably a best-seller book in the popular psychology and spiritual growth market. It has inspired millions of people and provided some meaning in an ever-complex social world. According to the American scholar of religion Wade Clark Roof (1999: 104), the reason people gave as to why this book was so important and personally transformative was located in the opening line, 'Life is difficult,' (itself Peck's own rendering of the first noble truth of Buddhism). The Baby Boomer American generation, struggling with the problems of a wealthy and excessive culture, with all the apparent privileges of the market society, were finding – as pictures of war and famine illuminated their living rooms – that their own lives were 'difficult'. M. Scott Peck provided hope for a meaning-hungry generation of western consumers and set the ground for their Generation-X children to find similar meaning in a media-saturated world. Whether intentional or not, M. Scott Peck's work insulated itself from the wider political problems of a 'difficult life' and addressed instead the narrower issues of personal development and well-being. His strategy was to draw on the resources of ancient traditions and offer the contours of an inner, psychological journey. But while many were being nourished on this appetite of self-awareness it is hard to imagine that the twentieth-century psychotherapeutic reconstruction of ancient insights was – perhaps unwittingly – imposing the language of privatisation. For all its success, M. Scott Peck was part of a North American psychologised world that ignored or at least downplayed the social and political aspects of life. According to Christopher Lasch (1980: 4) this turn to the individual was a key shift in North American culture in the 1970s:

After the political turmoil of the sixties, Americans have retreated to purely personal preoccupations. Having no hope of improving their lives in any of the ways that matter, people have convinced themselves that what matters is psychic self-improvement: getting in touch with their feelings, eating health food, taking lessons in ballet or belly-dancing, immersing themselves in the wisdom of the East, jogging, learning how to 'relate', overcoming the 'fear of pleasure'. Harmless in themselves, these pursuits, elevated to a program and wrapped in the rhetoric of authenticity and awareness, signify a retreat from politics and a repudiation of the recent past.

Despite often referring to the relationship between the microcosm and macrocosm of life, Peck reworked ancient religious insights and recast them in terms of the modern psychological self. Peck, for example, believed that mental health and spiritual growth required us to 'develop our own personal religion', that is one 'forged entirely through the fire of our questioning and doubting in the crucible of our own experience of reality' (Peck, 1990: 208). He argued that everyone has a religion whether they belong to a faith community or not. Religion is, in this sense, a personal 'worldview', often opposed to the 'dogmatic' traditions of one's parents. This reflects a significant trend in Anglo-American culture in the late twentieth century that has been crucial in the unhinging of the notion of 'spirituality' from 'the religions', namely, the notion that an individual can have their own private religion (or, as it is increasingly put, have their own inner 'spirituality'). This cultural phenomenon has been labelled 'Sheilaism' by the sociologist Robert Bellah (1985), after a Californian nurse who first expressed this idea to him.

Peck's message is one of self-discovery, but his resources are, ironically, the dogmatic insights, inherited traditions and religions of mothers and fathers. What is different is the packaging of such ideas in a psychological model, not the insights as such; so the Buddha's existential analysis of life as *dukkha* (suffering) becomes marketed in a much narrower psychological frame as *my own personal/private* 'life is difficult'. Rather than locate such thinking in the wider concerns of any specific tradition, we find a refashioning of Christianity,

Buddhism and Taoism in terms of the individual self (see Chapter Three). What is never raised is the possibility that the 'difficult life' is itself a result of the modern psychological understanding of the self in western consumer societies. Peck, for instance, explicitly argues that his own psychological insights are the same as those of the great religious founders:

> One way or another, these concepts have been set forth before – by Buddha, by Christ, by Lao-tse, among many others. The originality of this book results from the fact that I have arrived at their same meaning through the particular individual byways of my twentieth-century life. If you require greater understanding than these modern footnotes have to offer, then by all means proceed or return to the ancient texts.
>
> (Peck, 1990: 331)

In this chapter we do not wish to question the value that Peck's book and other popular classics, like *Chicken Soup for the Soul*, have had for many people. They have certainly provided some nourishment in a disillusioned world, but in our view they are palliative for the ills of a consumer society, rather than addressing the underlying social problems that create the need for such works in the first place. Many works of popular psychology and spirituality fail to draw attention to the wider processes that influence such writing, and never identify the political implications of a personal search that gives such priority to the individual over the social and the political. Peck's book is part of a whole spate of recent literature celebrating 'self'-styled answers to the challenges of life that play into the hands of modern capitalism. Indeed, *psychology as a modern discipline of the self is a political apparatus of modern society to develop and sustain consumers*. This is not to assume that psychology is part of direct government propaganda (although western governments support such research for military, educational and industrial purposes), but rather that psychology is a mechanism of a wider ideology of privatisation and individualisation. This process of psychologisation is not created by a few individuals and then implemented, but rather evolves through a set of institutional demands and historical forces. In post-war western society, social control is established through the legal, political and educational reinforcement of a private (consuming) self. In this sense, mass control and collectivism are not just features of fascist and communist societies. Rather they are reconfigured and hidden behind the capitalist doctrines of individual liberty and free choice. These different political regimes are certainly not oppressive in the same way or degree, but all socially control the individual for ideological reasons. *Psychological individualism is a new form of mass control within late capitalist society, creating a form of subjectivity built on ideals of consumer freedom.* It provides part of the philosophical infrastructure and rationale through which economic and political systems operate. This is not a conspiracy theory of government control, but rather a network of processes determined by the dominance of corporate ideology (Rose, 1990: 261–2). In this sense, the message of 'democratic freedom' and 'individualism' can hide the oppressive and abusive mechanisms of global corporate power.

Certain psychological models, and the institutions that sustain them, are pernicious and dangerous because they sustain models of being human that over-indulge ideas of an isolated self to the detriment of an awareness of social

> 'There is no such thing as society; there are individual men and women and there are families.'
>
> Margaret Thatcher, interview in *Woman's Own* magazine, 31 October 1987.

interdependence. The ideology of modern psychology supports the capitalist society of consumers, in which it originates, through the process of individualisation. The problem with individualism or privatisation is the way in which it constructs a person as a distinct unit – a kind of hermetically sealed and isolated self, as opposed to a relational and interdependent self. The difficult and challenging issue, especially in the compartmentalised world of modern western societies, is to recognise the interrelated nature of psychological knowledge and the material world. In this respect, we need to establish that questions about government oil reserves, land rights, deforestation and poverty are as important to personal well-being and a sense of self as the feel-good factors of a psychological self promoted in glossy magazines for café culture. Psychology, masking itself as a science, conceals its political role as the authorising ideology of individualism. The harsh reality is that few people, especially those benefiting from the situation, want to see the interconnected structures of psychology and capitalism. Even fewer want to recognise how the psychological individualism of capitalism creates on addiction to private spiritualities, offering short-term cures for contemporary social angst. Psychology sustains the ideology of individualism that is necessary for capitalism and consumerism to operate, and spirituality is the product of such a world, not a separate realm within it.

Spirituality in its privatised psychological formation is not a cure for our sense of social isolation and disconnectedness but is, in fact, part of the problem. Private spirituality, as opposed to an understanding of spirituality as linked to issues of social justice, is dangerous precisely because it conceals the underlying ideological effects of individualism. Psychologists rightly observe the problems of 'meaningless' values in consumer culture, but they unwittingly offer yet another consumer product as an answer to that void.

> 'Economics are the method. The object is to change the soul.'
>
> Margaret Thatcher, *The Sunday Times*, 7 May 1988.
>
> 'The distinctive marks of Christianity stem not from the social, but from the spiritual side of our lives.'
>
> Margaret Thatcher, 1988 address to the General Assembly of the Church of Scotland.

THE PSYCHOLOGISATION OF THE WESTERN WORLD

Since the birth of modern psychology with Wilhelm Wundt (1832–1920) and William James (1842–1910) in the 1870s, there has been a slow process of 'psychologising' human experience in the West. The process of 'psychologisation' is one in which human experience is understood in terms of the institutions and powers of a diverse range of 'psy' disciplines and knowledges that claim authority over previous models of being human (Rose, 1998: 104–5, 109ff). Before psychology, ways of thinking about the self were not always determined by the measurements of 'science' or by notions of a fixed essence to the self. Before psychology, the self was shaped by the philosophical imagination and (what we now call) 'religious' models of introspection. These allowed for more open-ended and fluid ideas about the self, due to the fact that identity was grounded in a divine reality or social group. Such traditions of thought also held onto the idea of an ineffable dimension to reality, something that could never be quantified by a narrow and calculative logic. In a world saturated with notions of a psychological self, it is difficult to imagine that there is an alternative. In other words, the psychological paradigm has become so naturalised – such a part of our everyday 'common-sense' – that it has established the basic conditions for thinking about modern subjectivity itself. In this context it is only by attention to history (how humans conceived of themselves *before* psychology) and careful attention to conceptions of the self in non-western cultures that one is even able to consider 'thinking beyond' or 'outside' the modern psychological self. In places where western psychological discourse has yet to infiltrate indigenous subjectivities, notions of a private self, existing in isolation from wider community relations, make little sense.

Western forms of the self constantly inscribe the language of private self and private possessions and actively subvert awareness of relational and social identity. Psychology carries this private and individualised self into its methods and measurements, a philosophical assumption that becomes a precondition of experimentation. It seeks to calculate and mark out a self for social ordering, production and consumption.

Psychology in its early years was a confused discipline in so far as much of what it could say was restricted to physiology and introspection, but it aspired to claims outside the limits of its analysis. Psychologists wrongly assumed that they could extend such knowledge into the wider cultural, linguistic and social spheres of life, realms that are not amenable to a natural science approach (where you can measure the object of knowledge). You cannot, for example, measure the nature of human beings like you can measure the nature of minerals. You can measure the *biological* aspects of human beings, but not their thoughts, language and imagination (which by definition defy measurement). However, the cultural climate for a measurable sense of what it was to be human meant that the physiological dimensions of psychological research created the illusion that it constituted a clearly defined 'science of man'. Philosophers since Immanuel Kant (1724–1804) had long realised that the human being escaped understanding according to a natural scientific method, but the philosophical and political aspects of psychology became hidden behind a wider politic focusing upon a practical utility of knowledge. The desire to find a 'science of man' is principally for the purposes of understanding, classifying and managing large masses of people in the terms dictated by society and the nation-state. However, there is no 'truth' of what it is to be human; rather, political ideologies assume that what a 'science' discovers somehow determines how things should be established. In philosophy this is known as the 'is–ought' fallacy – just because something is the case does not mean that something ought to result from it. Psychology is presented to us as a definitive 'science' of the human person, even though human beings have continually re-imagined themselves in each historical period and in different parts of the world in varied and complex ways.

Faltering between physiology, philosophy and politics, psychology branched into many directions, but continued to operate through a vision of the 'self' as a distinct unit, or closed system, to be examined and classified. Such knowledge increased the importance of private, individual experiences and placed emphasis upon ordering and understanding the individual subject according to an assumed 'truth' about what it is to be human. The issue for psychologists is to determine what they can and cannot say about human life, even though the discipline of psychology assumed authority in the twentieth century as the discourse of 'truth' about human beings.

Psychology was eventually adopted as the central ideology of western institutions, particularly welfare, educational and medical systems, and became a naturalised framework alongside political and economic forces in shaping the contemporary western world (and by extension elsewhere). The process of psychologisation has therefore been slowly carried out over a hundred years and reflects to a large degree the regime of modern 'governmentality' (or social organisation) and the reordering of the social-individual world. In the attempt to govern mass urban populations an effective system of ordering populations had to be established. The irony was that populations were ordered not through outwards signs of mass crowd control but through more detailed analysis of the human being, a hidden form of mass control. The power of controlling the world through the individual can be seen in a Buddhist parable about the invention of leather. The parable tells of a king who, so impressed by the discovery of leather and its softness to the touch, decreed that his entire kingdom should be covered in leather so that all of his subjects could enjoy its comfortable touch under foot. When this proved to be a task too grand for anyone to perform (not to mention the numbers of slaughtered cows required), an alternative was suggested – why not make shoes out of leather for each individual? Thus were leather shoes invented! This parable is used in the Buddhist tradition to emphasise the importance of working on the individual person in order to transform society. As we shall see, this is not because Buddhism is especially individualistic in its orientation, but rather that the tradition appreciated that the way to transform people is to do it on an individual level. At the level of social control this is exactly what psychology does. Psychology creates a 'subjectivity' (a sense of self) by 'subjecting' the self to the power of a normative understanding. According to Foucault, the networks of power in society create individual 'subjects' through a 'technique', or set of strategic relations. As he argues,

> This form of power applied itself to immediate everyday life which categorises the individual, marks him [sic] by his own individuality, attaches him to his own identity, imposes a law of truth on him which he must recognise.
>
> (Foucault, 1982: 212)

Psychology provides a way to organise society by categorising and ordering types and abilities. In education, for example, there was the invention of intelligence tests to differentiate groups within schools, in criminology there was the invention of the delinquent to monitor deviant behaviour, in psychiatry there was the creation of a diverse range of pathologies to arrange the 'normal' and 'abnormal', in counselling and therapy there was an ordering of the depressive personality to keep the excesses of an abusive culture at bay. Questioning the categories of psychology is not to diminish the physiological problems and levels of personal suffering that people have endured, but to question whether the classifications of psychology are neutral rather than political or social creations. Psychology organises the inner sense of the world by providing society with measurable tests for sexual, emotional and relational stresses.

According to capitalist ideology, if human beings can be measured and organised sufficiently then society will be transformed into an efficient mode of operation. Reaction times, levels of memory, skills of perception, rhythms of emotion could all be brought together to produce and to shape industrial output, assess educational ability and maintain social control. The efficient functioning of human beings would allow greater production and greater consumption and healthy 'individuals' would be manipulated to affirm their identity as a private, isolated self through the desire to consume. Psychological knowledge provided the structure for an economic order based upon the creation and promotion of individual desires. As such, it was a response to changes in the mechanisms of exchange in modern society. Complex populations require greater efficiency of supply to satisfy individual demands, and market processes are eased by having a model of humanity that could correspond to and even create desire. Human beings are exposed to many forms of propaganda and manipulation through advertising, but to be told 'who you were' and why you suffered was the ultimate panacea for the governance of potentially unruly populations. Psychology offers a complete narrative of human experience requiring only that the individual be located within its own language-world. It provides an apparent 'cure' for each individual, or at least offers a sedative of inner explanation. However, it is important to challenge the maps of the world offered by psychology as somehow the only 'truth' about being human and to question how psychological theories of the self support and benefit a wider political regime of knowledge.

Twentieth-century psychology is the emergence of a new power of governance or social organisation hiding in the clothes of an 'object-ive' science (achieved by the extension of its 'truth' beyond the limits of its initial physiological and empirical claims). It has received its greatest advancement in being aligned with the machinery of the mass media and neoliberalism, because the ideology of psychology could now be transmitted in an unrestricted form through ever-greater systems of distribution. Psychology mirrors the demands of society, and a society determined by the market will develop models of psychology suitable for its needs. Psychology is a model of understanding that attempts to anchor a 'truth' about being human in methodical study, but much of human life escapes this analysis. If psychology were a completely objective science then it could, as cognitive science and artificial intelligence aspires, eradicate the unruly and excessive demands of individuals and programme human beings accordingly. The fear of uncertainty in human beings makes the desire for a controlled understanding of human behaviour an understandable yearning, but being human is not something that can be put under the control of the machine, despite the attempts of psychology and political organisations. Psychology nonetheless is the regime of knowledge that dovetails with capitalism because its attempt to stabilise the self for the services of society is useful for law, order and the market. It is for this reason that psychology both shapes and is directed towards the ideology of the neoliberal world.

> Like much of the rest of everyday neoliberal life, professional psychology is now resolutely consumer-orientated. Along with the former passengers who are now 'customers' of railway companies, the academics who have become 'content providers' and the patients who have metamorphosed into 'clients', so too the APA (American Psychological Association) has begun to describe itself as a 'consumer advocacy organisation' . . . Psychology and psychologists are now everywhere, and not always where you might expect.
>
> (Hansen *et al.*, 2003: 25, 33)

If human beings can be known they can be controlled and, even if they cannot be fully known in rationalist terms, transmitting the illusion of knowing will at least contribute to the management of large sections of society. The problem for psychology and rationalists alike is that some traditions of thinking, often designated as religious in nature, have held that knowledge about human beings cannot be placed into neat boxes. According to such traditions, some aspects of life exceed the limits of rational comprehension and calculation. Indeed, in some cases our everyday views of the world and the self are themselves said to be shaped by powerful illusions about the self, requiring rigorous discipline and vigilance to uproot. The scientific discipline of psychology, however, has largely forgotten its fragile foundations and also the roots of its own speculations in the traditions that it now disavows. As William James recognised, our ideas about ourselves are varied, and we are always faced with the 'More' which exceeds our understanding:

> We must frankly recognise the fact that we live in partial systems, and that parts are not interchangeable in the spiritual life . . . We must begin by using less particularised terms; and, since one of the duties of the science of religions is to keep religion in connection with the rest of science, we shall do well to seek first of all a way of describing the 'More' which psychologists may also recognise as real.
>
> (James, [1902] 2002: 377, 394)

The Psychologisation of Religion or the Invention of 'Religious Experience'

The success of psychology as a totalising (scientific) discourse of human life lies in providing a view of humanity that can offer explanations of the most banal to the most sublime. On the one hand, it provides a kind of fashion of the self with psychological quizzes about relationships to satisfy the numbed existence of consumption and, on the other hand, it attempts to offer explanations of the most mysterious events from near-death experiences to mystical consciousness. *Psychology has an explanation for everything because it locates the sources of everything within the self.* The paradox of psychology is that it is human beings who have created the method of viewing and analysing the human self that we call psychology, and they too are subject to the same illusions and delusions that they analyse in their study of human behaviour and experience.

Historically, of course, psychological theories are shown to be full of inaccuracies, and new models are superimposed as corrections, only to be later discarded when the next fashionable, new theory emerges on the scene. This provisional nature of psychological 'truth' is not simply (as some psychologists would like to argue) a matter of improving techniques and accuracy, rather, it reflects the shifting political sense of what it is to be human and the adaptation of psychological 'science' to fit such shifts. Psychological theories, as we have noted, tend to mirror the political climate; for instance, cognitive 'science' mirrors the growing importance of information technology and the uniformity of global finance-based capitalism. The desire to know and control the human being results in ever-new ways of mapping the interior sense of the self for social and political utility.

Psychology, not surprisingly, ventured into the territory of religion as it sought to psychologise all aspects of life (and death). From the very foundations of psychology there were attempts to explain and describe religious experiences. Conversion, mysticism, dogma, meditation, prayer, pastoral care and religious images have all been examined and translated into psychological events from a variety of different methodological perspectives, from psychoanalysis to neuroscience. The twentieth century is witness to the slow assimilation of the religious into the psychological. As psychology has become more enmeshed in market values and economic control there has been an infiltration of the spirit of capitalism into religious discourse. *The key part of this assimilation can be found in the construction of the modern idea of spirituality.* The integration of psychological discourse into the realm of spirituality is an example of the psychologisation of religion in the service of capitalist ideology. Indeed, today the shift from interest in the 'psychology of religion' (which offers the potential of a critical and historical understanding) to contemporary 'spirituality' is witness to the success of the internalisation of private models of religion founded upon psychological constructions of the human. Modern forms of spirituality hide the underlying political-psychological implications of this regime of knowledge. As Wade Clarke Roof (1999: 109) has suggested,

> when spirituality is recast in strictly psychological terms, it is often loosened from its traditional moorings – from historic creeds and doctrines, from broad symbolic universes, from religious community. There is narrative enmeshment, but in its specificity and inward focus the communal dimension so important historically to cultivating spirituality is weakened.

It is important to realise that, unlike challenges from the natural sciences in physics and chemistry, psychology has on the whole – with some pockets of resistance – been a useful companion for Christianity (indeed it is arguably born out of Christian history). Psychology developed much older traditions of introspection within western culture and offered the promise of an internal reordering of the Christian message for an individualised and secularised world. However, in the demand for a 'science' of the self, psychology distanced itself from the trappings of a 'religious self' and sought to offer ideas of being human on a reductionist and measurable basis. This separation of religion and psychology required the disarming of much of the cultural heritage that had given birth to psychology in the first place. The careful documentation of the self according to models of experimentation and empirical observation, taken from the natural sciences, concealed the underlying philosophical and religious assumptions of the discipline. Carefully concealed behind the apparatus of measurement and new technical linguistic formulations, such speculations were made to appear as *factual* analysis. Scientific psychology, however, still operated according to assumptions about the self and introspection that had already been long established within the Christian tradition from Augustine. At the same time, there were areas of psychology that became disillusioned with a purely reductionist approach to studying human experience, and there were those who sought to explore the insights of the religious traditions for the services of psychology. Psychology, however much the discipline and its practitioners tried to escape the confines of the history of religions, has continually returned to the limits of its discourse and opened up enigmatic questions that no science can hope to answer – questions about the meaning of human existence, the fragility of life and its human narratives.

Psychological knowledge appropriated religious ideas for the services of the social-political institutions. It established a form of thought-control by turning religious discourse into private and individualised constructions, which pacified the social, and potentially revolutionary, aspects of religion. Under the terms set by political liberalism, religion could exist in the modern secular state so long as it was pushed safely into the private sphere. One way to achieve this is by containing it within psychological registers of meaning that would thereby limit the possibilities of its threat to ruling elites. Religion in the USA, for instance, is celebrated and welcomed precisely because it is largely pacified by a logic of privatisation that does not threaten the personal 'freedoms' of the business enterprise and the machinery of government, while religion as practised in Iran remains threatening to the West because its understanding of the human being is determined by Islamic constructions of self and society and has not been subjected to the same degree of infiltration by the pacifying forces of western psychology. The psychologised self is therefore one of the political spaces through which religious knowledge is reordered for the modern liberal state. In effect, psychology sought to cure the ills of society by adopting its own psychologised religion of the self. The contemporary celebration of spirituality by psychologists is a sign of how far the process of psychologisation has gone in pacifying the more unruly and challenging aspects of the religious traditions. Psychology distilled the social revolutionary aspects of religion to form a privatised religion rendered amenable to the demands of neoliberal ideology. Thus, the anxieties of the French sociologist Émile Durkheim about the loss of the social cohesiveness provided by community-oriented religions seems to have been fulfilled:

> If one does not want to be open to grave misunderstanding it is necessary to be aware of confusing a free, private, optional religion, fashioned according to one's own needs and understanding, with a religion handed down by tradition, formulated by a whole group and which is obligatory to practise. The two disciplines which are so different cannot meet the same needs; one is completely orientated towards the individual, the other towards society.
>
> (Émile Durkheim, cited in Pickering, 1975: 96)

The introduction of psychology into the realm of 'the religious' has, on the whole, not been a threatening activity for psychology because it is not the product of a creative dialogue with the religious traditions themselves. Rather, it is a reordering of the religious in terms of the modern notion of 'spirituality' by the discipline of psychology on behalf of its political and economic partners. The tragic side of this process is that those who uphold the virtues of a private spirituality believe that it represents the salvaging of an ethical and transcendent dimension in a materialist and rationalist culture gone mad. In reality, however, such privatised spiritualities operate as a form of thought-control that supports the ideology of late capitalism. 'Spirituality' is the conceptual space that suggests the promotion of wholesome ethical values, but only by perpetuating a form of ethical myopia that turns our attention away from social injustice. It does this by turning the social ethic of religion into a private reality for self-comfort and self-consumption. But how did this process begin in the history of psychology?

The Privatisation of Religion

The engagement of psychology with religion is, on the whole, the history of the privatisation of religion and the reconfiguration of religion in terms of the private, psychological self. This shift in religious understanding has, unwittingly in some cases, and intentionally in others, played into the hands of a neoliberal ideology of religion. It has removed the social dimension of religion and created a spirituality of the self – of the consuming self. The history of psychology and religion since the 1890s has been one where religious 'experience' has become an individual event and where the boundaries of the self have been reinforced. Building on Protestant notions of the self in relation to God – and thus continuing longer historical processes of individualisation from the Reformation – the early psychologists of religion located the significance of religion within individual experience. Religious experiences, predominantly Christian in nature, were internalised as private events. Religious conversion could now be seen as related to changes during puberty and adolescence, God could be seen as a projection of infant fantasies, mysticism could be reconfigured as the pursuit of 'altered states of consciousness' and religious practices became represented as manifestations of inner psychical processes rather than as social forms of expression. While this method of analysis provided many insights into the internal world of human subjectivity, it also created a distorted picture of the 'religious' world as a whole. It not only created a set of experiences understood to be constitutive of religious experience, as opposed to other experiences, it also falsely assumed that you could separate the individual from the social. As Erich Fromm (1978: 52) has shown in his own correlation of religion, psychology and society: 'The history of religion gives ample evidence of this correlation between social structure and kinds of religious experience.'

The psychologisation of religion – turning religion into a psychological event – is then an ideological process through which an internal economy of the self is set above an external economy of social relations. This internal economy of religion found in psychology mirrored the economy of self-interest dominating the western world. In this sense, the history of western psychology cannot be separated from the history of western capitalism. The privatisation of religion through psychology provided the platform for later markets exploring the private world of spiritualities to flourish. The historical process of this transformation is complex and is part of the wider separation of the social and individual at the turn of the twentieth century. While it is too simple to see sociology as the space for left-wing thinking and psychology as the space for right-wing thinking, there are nonetheless important features of these disciplinary domains that played into ideological structures beyond their own purview. To understand how the privatisation of religion in psychology was taken up by neoliberal capitalism in the late twentieth century requires us briefly to sketch some of the key theoretical moments in this history.

William James and the Privatisation of Mysticism

One of the key thinkers to set the agenda for the psychology of religion was undoubtedly William James (1842–1910) and his seminal work *The Varieties of Religious Experience* (1902). In this book, James established a psychological framing of religion, and even though he was aware of the limitations of his method, and clearly outlined the 'arbitrary' and provisional nature of his approach, those who followed him almost universally fashioned religious experience in his terms, but without the caveats. While James talked of 'pattern-setters' within religious traditions, he did not realise that he would become a 'pattern-setter' for understanding religious experience in the twentieth century, shaping 'New Age' jargon and providing the mechanisms for rethinking religion in terms of individual private experience. James, influenced by Protestant readings of religious experience and his father's Swedenborgian heritage, was the originator of modern psychological conceptions of spirituality. He openly acknowledged that he ignored the social dimensions of religion and gave priority to states of mind and inner feelings. While James cannot be held responsible for the later utilisation of his thinking, the approach he adopted was captured by later generations enjoying the benefits of free-market spirituality, which celebrated the individual.

> At the outset we are struck by one great partition which divides the religious field. On the one side of it lies institutional, on the other personal religion . . . I propose to ignore the institutional branch entirely, to say nothing of the ecclesiastical organization, to consider as little as possible the systematic theology and the ideas about gods themselves, and to confine myself as far as I can to personal religion pure and simple . . . Religion, therefore, as I now ask you arbitrarily to take it, shall mean for us *the feelings, acts, and experiences of individual men in their solitude*, so far as they apprehend themselves to stand in relation to whatever they may consider the divine.
>
> (James, 2002: 28–30, our underlining.)

One of the key moments in the privatisation of religion that James established was the construction of mysticism in terms of private, intense feelings. The history of mysticism, as later scholars have shown (Jantzen, 1995; King, 1999a), does not support these psychological renderings of experience, but James's 'restriction' of the term (which he openly acknowledged as a restriction for the purposes of analysis) created the modern construction of mysticism as a private, intense experience.

> The words 'mysticism' and 'mystical' are often used as terms of mere approach, to throw at any opinion which we regard as vague and vast and sentimental, and without a base in either facts or logic . . . So, to

keep it *useful by restricting it*, I will do what I did in the case of the word 'religion', and simply propose to you four marks which, when an experience has them, may justify us in calling it mystical for the purpose of the present lectures . . . 1. Ineffability . . . 2. Noetic quality . . . 3. Transiency . . . 4. Passivity . . . These four characteristics are sufficient to mark out a group of *states of consciousness* peculiar enough to deserve a special name and to call for careful study. Let it then be called the mystical group.

(James, 2002: 294–5, our emphasis)

After James and the spiritualists, the focus on states of consciousness came to dominate the psychology of religion and paved the way for a spirituality of inner consciousness. James, of course, did not bring about this transformation single-handedly, it was the development of his work by his followers, such as James Pratt (1875–1944) and, more specifically, a later generation of scholars including Gordon Allport (1897–1967) and Abraham Maslow (1908–70), who propagated an individualised understanding of religion within North American culture. It would be wrong to assume that these thinkers deliberately developed a psychology of religion for capitalism. It is rather the case that their psychology emerged in a context of a North American economic climate that celebrated the individual pursuit of wealth. Psychological ideologies flourished in such conditions. Maslow's psychology, for instance, did not reflect the Two-Thirds World or the land of his parents in Eastern Europe. Rather, it was the psychology of an affluent society that could separate out a hierarchy of needs where 'spirituality' could be separated from the basic needs of finding food, shelter and water to live. The cumulative effect of this was the emergence of a religious experience tailored for wealthy individuals rather than for social justice. Religious experience, in part at least, reflects the economic conditions in which it emerges, and psychology provided one of the mechanisms of individualisation that bridges religion and capitalism in a neoliberal world.

The privatisation of religion was not just a North American phenomenon, although it received its greatest support in that culture, it was part of the wider western psychological world. Sigmund Freud

(1856–1939) and Carl Jung (1875–1961) also brought religious experience into the inner world, although arguably they were also struggling with anthropological baggage and collective processes. Freud and Jung in many ways reflect the problems of establishing a psychology of religion separate from other disciplines, as both men ventured into the tensions of the social and psychic, with ideas of an 'archaic heritage' (Freud) and a 'collective unconscious' (Jung). They nonetheless both provided psychological models for a later generation of thinkers who reduced everything to a private, psychic reality and an individualised market of 'New Age' consumers. Jung, for example, directly linked the spiritual with the psychical world.

> To me, the crux of the spiritual problem of today is to be found in the fascination which psychic life exerts upon modern man. If we are pessimists, we shall call it a sign of decadence; if we are optimistically inclined, we shall see in it the promise of a far-reaching spiritual change in the Western world. At all events, it is a significant manifestation.
>
> (Jung, 1984: 251)

It was however the development of humanistic psychology in the USA that had the greatest impact in forging the modern, privatised sense of spirituality. Humanistic psychology, or 'Third Force' psychology as it is sometimes known, sought to overcome the negative features of behaviourism and psychoanalysis in a move that captured the optimism of North American self-expression. As Don Browning (1987: 64) has suggested: 'The cultural power and attractiveness of humanistic psychology are partially explained by its continuity with significant strands of individualism that have characterised American history.'

Humanistic psychology later evolved into transpersonal psychology, or what has become known as 'Fourth Force' psychology, completing the cycle of turning religion into a consumer product of the self and shaping a spirituality for the market. Transpersonal psychology maintains some of the technical language of religion, but locates such experiences in human potential and states of consciousness. It plays with ideas of transcendence, awareness and the spiritual, but frames them as psychological not religious questions. This is a long way from William James's careful enquiry and, in the slow process of dislocating the institutional, the social and the traditional disciplines of religion, a new configuration of 'spirituality' has been created. Spirituality is now a private, psychological event that refers to a whole range of experiences floating on the boundary of religious traditions. The very difficulty with defining spirituality, as we saw in the last chapter, reflects this gathering together of varied experiences and trends, such as transpersonal psychology. The lack of specificity allows it to be effective in the marketplace and reduces its concern for social ethics and cultural location. While transpersonal psychology seeks to go 'beyond ego' it still reinforces the *private* state of consciousness and often uncritically reflects the values of individualism rather than the wider social domain (Lee and Marshall 2003). Transpersonal psychology rarely becomes transformative of the social, even though there were trends to correct some of the aspects of an individualistic psychology. In transpersonal psychology spirituality emerges as a product of religious fragmentation and eclecticism, hidden in the psychological structures of individualism. It is a box without content, because the content has been thrown out and what is left is a set of psychological descriptions with no referent. There is no referent because, in order to substantiate the ideas, one requires an explanatory cosmology that makes sense of the individual's place in the world and not a market brand name or a set of abstract ideas extracted from older traditions. Transpersonal psychology, despite its considerable promise as an antidote to psychological individualism, provides little evidence of an orientation to the collective. The interiorised transcendence that its proponents tend to offer does little to challenge structural violence and inequality and does little more than provide another avenue for inventing the self in capitalist society. Anthony Sutich's early definition of 'transpersonal psychology' reflects this privatisation of the spiritual.

The emerging 'Fourth Force' (Transpersonal Psychology) is concerned specifically with the scientific study and responsible implementation of becoming, individual and species-wide meta-needs, ultimate values,

unitive consciousness, peak experiences, B values, ecstasy, mystical
experience, awe, being, self-actualisation, essence, bliss, wonder,
ultimate meaning, transcendence of the self, spirit, oneness, cosmic
awareness, individual and species-wide synergy, maximal
interpersonal encounter, sacralization of everyday life, transcendental
phenomena; cosmic self, humor and playfulness; maximal sensory
awareness, responsiveness and expression; and related concepts,
experiences and activities.

(Sutich, 1969: 77–8)

HUMANISTIC PSYCHOLOGY AND THE PRIVATISATION
OF SPIRITUALITY

In 1950, the Harvard psychologist Gordon Allport advanced the
privatisation of religion in his work *The Individual and His Religion*. In
attempting to develop a positive religious sentiment, Allport upheld
the American values of democracy and freedom of choice to create
an engagement with religion that allowed a rejection of tradition and
the cultivation of individual personality as a new religious space.
Developing the work of Friedrich Schleiermacher, William James
and Rudolf Otto, Allport rejected institutional religion in order to
develop a subjective religious attitude. The key part of Allport's project
was a gradual erosion of the traditional institutions of ('immature')
religion to be replaced by a private ('mature' and 'healthy') religion.
Psychology provided the 'scientific' legitimation for translating the
religious world into a concern for individual health and maturity.
This shift away from institutional religion was not just a method
of approach as it was for James, it was now fast becoming a question
of pathology. The privatisation of religion was the shift in power from
the Church to the state apparatus of psychology. The force of religion
was taken away from the religious institutions and given over to
market forces. Allport was another point along the road to a private
spirituality, which would flourish in a consumerist climate. Allport
gives priority to 'individual' meaning, as he states:

One underlying value judgement flavours my writing. It is a value that
to my mind every supporter of democracy must hold: the right of each

individual to work out his own philosophy of life to find his personal niche in creation, as best he can. His freedom to do so will be greater if he sees clearly the forces of culture and conformity that invite him to be content with a merely second-hand and therefore for him, with an immature religion. It is equally essential to his freedom of choice that he understand the pressures of scorn and intimidation that tend to discourage his religious quest altogether.

(Allport, 1962: vii–viii)

The greatest shift towards private spirituality, however, can be seen in the work of Abraham Maslow, particularly as his work was picked up by the 1960s Hippie culture and dovetailed with the psychedelic world of Aldous Huxley and Timothy Leary. In this atmosphere, 'spirituality' became a product, like a drug, to change consciousness and lifestyle and provide happiness amidst the economic boom of North American life. Maslow's work did more for 'New Age' spirituality products and their capitalisation than most psychological theories, principally because he created a new terminology for 'religious experience', which effectively divorced it from 'religious tradition'. His ideas of 'self-actualisation', 'peak-experience', 'Being-cognition' and 'transpersonal psychology' have all played a key part in the creation of capitalist spiritualities. His language facilitated a clear break of 'spirituality' from its institutional moorings, and opened the space for spirituality to be seen as a 'secular' rather than an especially 'religious' phenomenon.

Maslow reinforced the private, intense model of religious expression that James had constructed half a century earlier. Conducting his analysis of experience according to his already developed model of 'spiritual' experience and sampling disillusioned college graduates, Maslow would ask his interviewees about their ecstatic and rapturous moments in life, not realising that religious insight often came from experiences of suffering and denial. This feel-good spirituality of the self was part of the wider process of turning the social ideals of religion into the interiorised world of the self, what we have called the 'psychologisation of religion'. The predetermined nature of Maslow's exploration can be seen in the framing of his questions:

I would like you to think of the most *wonderful* experience or experiences of your life; *happiest* moments, *ecstatic* moments, moments of *rapture*, perhaps from being in love, or from listening to music or suddenly 'being-hit' by a book or a painting, or from some great creative moment. First list these. And then try to tell me how you feel in such *acute* moments, how you feel differently from the way you feel at other times, how you are at the moment a *different* person in some ways.

(Maslow, 1976: 67, our emphasis)

Maslow's psychology was built on the principle of positive motivation towards a healthy realisation of human potential. Like inflation and deflation of the markets, people could reach 'growth' motivation in the realisation of love and self-esteem, but much of this echoed the privileges of a wealthy culture, and his famous 'hierarchy of needs' was more a hierarchy of 'capitalist wants'. It reflected a culture where basic physiological needs were excessively fulfilled and even of secondary concern, allowing for the 'higher' expressions of cognition, aestheticism and self-realisation. This partition of expression clearly ignored the rich traditions of other cultures where poverty and denial brought about transformation. This was a spiritual message for a culture of excess and one that rejected the shared expression of communal religious faith. It was the birth of a private religion based on individual 'peak-experiences'. Thus, according to Maslow (1976: 27–8):

the evidence from the peak-experience permits us to talk about the essential, the intrinsic, the basic, the most fundamental religious or transcendent experience as a *totally private and personal one* which can hardly be shared (except with other 'peakers'). As a consequence, all the paraphernalia of organised religion – buildings and specialised personnel, rituals, dogmas, ceremonials, and the like – are to the 'peaker' secondary, peripheral, and of doubtful value in relation to the intrinsic and essential religious or transcendent experience. Perhaps they may even be very harmful in various ways. From the point of view of the peak-experiencer, each person has his own *private religion*, which he develops out of his own *private revelations* in which are revealed to him his own *private myths and symbols, rituals and ceremonials*, which may be of the profoundest meaning to him personally and yet completely idiosyncratic, i.e. of no meaning to anyone else. But to say it even more simply, each 'peaker' discovers, develops, and retains his own religion.

(our emphasis)

Religious traditions, according to Maslow, no longer have the exclusive right to talk about unseen worlds and hidden depths of meaning, or even their own intellectual and cultural expression. Maslow extrapolated the insights of religious traditions and reworked them into psychological ideas. In so doing, he transformed an ostensibly 'religious' phenomenon into a 'secular' product, which survives today in 'New Age' magazines and corporate business personal development programmes. After Maslow, spirituality became the new addiction of the educated, white middle classes, something that showed a rejection of the abuses associated with traditional religion but which celebrated freedom and individual expression. Privatised spirituality emerges here as the new *cultural prozac* bringing transitory feelings of ecstatic happiness and thoughts of self-affirmation, but never addressing sufficiently the underlying problem of social isolation and injustice. In an environment where many experience a lack of meaning in their lives, spirituality offers a cultural sedative providing individual rapture. What is masked behind this addiction to private religion is the way in which it exacerbates the problems of meaning associated with materialism and individualism in the very desire for some kind of escape from the world. Such capitalist spiritualities thereby end up reinforcing the very problems that many of its advocates seek to overcome.

The irony of Maslow's work, as with Allport's psychological theories, is that the very rejection of religion and the appeal to a private religion relied upon the adoption of another authority and another system of constraint. In the very act of freeing the mind from the dogma of religion, consumers now entered the thought-control of individualism. As we saw earlier, while many see the individualism embedded in psychology as part of its freedom from social control, this has prevented them from seeing how individualism is also a key element in the market creation and control of human desires. The assumption that 'psychological individualism' provides greater freedom or a more effective means of social organisation needs to be questioned. Once the individual is abstracted from the interrelated needs of the wider community, their individualism becomes a site for political and economic control. Rejection of the Church, the synagogue and the temple is replaced by the new authoritarianism of the market and capital. Spiritual self-actualisation is a market-actualisation, clever for its very concealment. While 'New Age' followers dance the gospel of self-expression they service the financial agents and chain themselves to a spirituality of consumerism. While they selectively ravage the feel-good fabric of ancient cultural and religious traditions, their disciplines and practices can easily isolate them from the resources of social justice and community to be found within those same traditions. The ancient religious traditions of the world, of course, are not without their own dark histories of thought-control, oppression and violence. Nevertheless, what they also offer are ways to overcome the pernicious consequences of individualism, self-interest and greed throughout history. The illusion of religious free expression in private spirituality is the prison of capitalism, because it fails to acknowledge the interdependence of self within community and the ethical necessity of countering the abuses of power within market societies. It restricts the individual to a unit of consumption rather than a dynamic of relation and creative expression.

Maslow's idea of a 'spirituality' of mutated religious ideas is welcomed by the business world for its motivational qualities. Indeed, at one point Maslow spent time at the Non-Linear Systems Inc. plant in Del Mar, California, and wrote in glowing terms about the effectiveness of his ideas for corporate culture. This application of his work

> 'Because we have freed ourselves of the older overt forms of authority, we do not see that we have become the prey of a new kind of authority. We have become automatons who live under the illusion of being self-willing individuals.'
>
> Erich Fromm, *The Fear of Freedom*, Routledge, [1942] 2001, p. 218.

continues today and illustrates how a Maslovian spirituality joins forces with the business world. Spirituality, once deeply entwined in cosmologies that related the individual to society and the cosmos as a whole, is now dissected and decontextualised for corporate capitalism. The silent takeover of religion is accomplished through this psychologisation and, through this process, market forces encroach upon yet another area of human life. As Deborah Stephens (2000: viii) poignantly notes:

> the reason Maslow matters today, nearly three decades after his death, is precisely because of places like Silicon Valley . . . As we embrace innovation and human capital as prime factors in competitive advantage, Maslow matters more today than when he lived.

POPULAR PSYCHOLOGY AND CAPITALIST SPIRITUALITY

In the attempt to understand religion from a 'scientific' psychological point of view, with all the restrictions upon its methodology, psychology has produced a new 'religion' of the self (Vitz, 1977). This religion of the self is effective because of its allegiance to the free market of individual choice. Economists, from Adam Smith onwards, have realised that you need an underlying model of the self in order to facilitate market forces. The political and economic structures allow private forms of spirituality to integrate with consumerism. As the media transmit ideas of private spirituality, so the quest for an individual meaning to be purchased and consumed reinforces the sense that spirituality is indeed private and individualistic. Psychology provides a way for the market to embrace religion through the language of 'spirituality' and politically removes its threat to the status quo. In effect, the territorial takeover of religion by psychology (individualisation) is the platform for the takeover of spirituality by capitalism (corporatisation). As we shall see in Chapter Four, this is not a completely smooth transition. Nevertheless, 'heroic individualism' is the framework through which the entrepreneurial culture of the 1980s emerged. Psychology makes religion into a product for private consumption and, as the fabric of the old institutions crumble, so the alienated masses start to worship at the new altar of capitalism, even when it is dressed in the outer garments of traditional religion. It is not, as Fromm indicates, a question of religion or not, 'but which kind of religion, whether it is one furthering man's development, the unfolding of his specifically human powers, or one paralyzing them' (Fromm, 1978: 26).

The problems with this psychological-capitalist spirituality are numerous, both in terms of appreciating psychology and its limits and in terms of social ethics. The investment in psychology provided, as we have stated, a framework for governing society, but the values of psychological methods of hypothesis-testing and empiricism have been lost in its enslavement to ideological models of individualism. Psychology can only have value today if it recognises its limits as a science, not by assuming ontological rights over the nature of human beings in its philosophical and political adventures. One of the central problems of psychology has been its adoption of a closed self, which it assumes is scientifically given rather than socially created. Theories of perception, memory and cognition, for example, operate on this notion of a closed system, but such unified models of the self conceal the divided self of social inequality and the multiple selves of our social and linguistic functioning. The illusion of a unified self is the market subject, the consuming agent, necessary for the function of late capitalistic markets. Its illusion is that the self somehow exists in isolation, when it is in fact a product of a complex network of economic, political, cultural and social interactions. Moreover, in its self-description as an objective 'science', psychology as a discipline has refused to acknowledge not only its own intellectual debts – namely, the pre-modern cultural heritage that constitutes its formative history, but also its own social location.

One of the problems of private, psychologised spirituality is the way in which it reinforces the idea that the individual is solely responsible for his or her own suffering. It supports a world where meaning is a private reality and where individuals make sense of their lives in isolation – a self-styled and custom-built spirituality purchased in the marketplace – rather than one generated through the social and historical lines of transmission within communities. However, the private spirituality supported by psychology is a collective political reality offering an ideology of separation. This ideology of privatisation breaks the social self and conceals, as we have noted, the collective manipulation of 'isolated individuals' in the language of free will and choice. When spirituality is built upon such a model it becomes locked into isolating practices that alienate people from each other and from moral responsibility for the collective good. While not denying the reality of the individual agent, it is important to realise the many and varied ways in which such agency remains intrinsically woven together with that of other human beings in terms of language, culture and identity. To overcome the alienating practices of psychologised spirituality, it is necessary to challenge the boundaries between self and other and to recognise the importance of interdependence. In recent years, following work in social psychology and social constructivism in the 1970s, there has been a group of psychologists who have started to critically examine the discipline and practices of psychology. They attempt to identify the social and political context of psychological thought and rethink the subject according its cultural determinants and its relation to social justice. They even question the foundations and possibility of psychology as conventionally conceived (see, for example, Sloan, 2000 and Carrette, 2001). This approach has become known as 'critical' psychology and has allowed for a rethinking of the discipline in terms of the politics of knowledge. It is now possible to see how psychology supports the political regime of capitalism by providing a model of humanity premised upon individualism, privatisation and a closed self. Political ideologies and economic regimes carry with them an underlying philosophy of being human and the correspondence between the history of psychology and capitalism bears witness to such an alliance. The political critique of psychology also results in questioning any simple reduction of individual suffering to our private psychological world and rejects the separation of our sense of self from the contributing social and economic factors. As David Smail has so powerfully demonstrated,

> The ills we suffer are not consequent upon our personal inadequacies or moralistically attributed faults; they are the inevitable result of publicly endorsed and communally practised forms of indifference, greed and exploitation, and require a moral reformation of our public, not our private ways of life.
>
> (Smail 1998: 152)

The psychologised forms of spirituality that have developed over the last century attempt to locate meaning within the individual according to a selective valuing of intense experiences within the self and a closed system of cognition. Practitioners within the mental health field, for instance, often appeal to the need of western societies to appreciate the spiritual side of patients and clients in a world where materialist and rationalist judgements prevail. They believe that this search for the 'spiritual' within each person will counter the abuses of a wider instrumentalism and materialism. However, while there are important and valuable dimensions to such 'holistic' approaches in providing personal integration, meaning and a sense of value, the privatised and individualistic aspects of such practices can often conceal the social and political realities that are carried forward in its palliative, pastoral message. Spirituality, in this way, can easily become a virtuous, if somewhat deluded, attempt to deal with the 'whole' person, but still in rather isolated terms. In a similar way, 'New Age' groups argue that traditional religions have failed and new forms of spirituality should be embraced to unite people to the earth, to the cosmic reality and to hidden mystical powers. Unfortunately, this appeal is misguided if it fails to understand the political forces behind the will-to-power of psychological 'truth'. As 'New Age' followers and healthcare practitioners uphold 'spirituality' as a way out of oppressive material worlds, they can paradoxically reinscribe the forces of isolation by focusing upon the individual. The isolation provides, as Parker (1997: 133) has identified, the basis for ideologically shaping the individual:

> Our experience of ourselves as separate and isolated from other people means that we have particularly hostile and fearful relationships with others, and these feelings are exaggerated when we relate to those in authority. The beliefs that we have deep down about our own nature and about those lesser and greater than ourselves are forms of *ideology*.

Late capitalist societies operate upon the mechanisms of social isolation. They create a social vacuum and an individualised sense of emptiness that consumerism promises, but intrinsically fails, to satisfy. In such a situation, *salvation through the spirituality market covertly provides new resources for sustaining the materialistic culture that they are ostensibly seeking to resist.*

The introduction of 'private' models of spirituality can be a dangerous move, especially in the helping professions and pastoral care. In the very desire to cure the addictions of modern living, patients are offered models of 'spirituality' to provide greater meaning in an empty world. This capitalist spirituality, however, only increases private consumer addiction. It offers personalised packages of meaning and social accommodation rather than recipes for social change and identification with others. In this sense, capitalist spirituality is the psychological sedative for a culture that is in the process of rejecting the values of community and social justice. The cultural hegemony of this kind of spirituality grows as market forces increase and as neo-liberal ideology is unhindered in its takeover of all aspects of human life and meaning. The desire for more diverse forms of spirituality to counter the ideology of consumption increases with the ever-perpetuating production line of new 'spiritual' products. The vacuous nature of the 'spiritual' marketplace creates a greater demand and need for some kind of 'real', 'pure' or 'authentic' spiritual experience, always just out of reach, like the inner contentment that consumerism promises but never fulfils. The consumer world of 'New Age' spirituality markets 'real', 'pure' or 'authentic' spiritual experiences, but these are manufactured worlds that seek to escape the 'impure' political reality of spirituality. The problem is always to identify which ideology is constructing and informing the idea of spirituality at any particular point in history. Capitalist spirituality only raises the desire for ever-new versions of spirituality that reinforce our private and isolated worlds. In the end, such spiritualities are too easily co-opted by the desiring machine of consumerism. Writing in 1970, Erich Fromm (1995: 67) had already appreciated that

Man [*sic*] is in the process of becoming a *homo consumens*, a total consumer. This image of man almost has the character of a new religious vision in which heaven is just a big warehouse where everyone can buy something new every day, indeed, where he [*sic*] can buy everything that he wants and even a little more than his neighbour. This vision of the total consumer is indeed a new image of man that is conquering the world, quite regardless of the differences of political organisation and ideology.

What we are calling, respectively, *individualist/consumerist* and *corporatist/capitalist* spiritualities devalue embodied communities by increasing the self-importance of individuality (or the corporation) and placing the pursuit of individual (and/or corporate) wealth above social justice. These forms of spirituality are the result of a failure to recognise that individuality is born out of community and that 'spirituality', as a psychological reality, is a hidden form of social manipulation of the same order as oppressive forms of thought-control associated with religious traditions in previous eras. More importantly, what such forms of spirituality leave behind in their distillation of the spiritual from the religious are the resources of social conscience and community identity that those traditions provided for humanity.

Socially engaged forms of spirituality do not eradicate a concern for the individual, but rather reject the idea that the individual is a separate entity to be measured for the purposes of social control and consumption. As some forms of 'critical psychology' have emphasised, the individual is always social. The individual sense of self reflects and shapes the social world, either in the negative form of isolation or in a positive form as social integration. Socially engaged forms of spirituality recognise that the sense of self must be built on social networks, not on private separation and individual consumption. As Stanczak and Miller (2002: 24) have identified in a recent report on *Engaged Spirituality*: 'spirituality only becomes enacted for social transformation when the spiritual experiences find personal resonance with motivations and available patterns of action for bringing about social change'. Such engaged approaches locate spirituality and individual identity within the social fabric, and recognise that our sense of personal worth is grounded upon social value and relationship, not upon private gratification and individual possession. When the individual self is seen as a node in a web of social relations, one can see the need for pastoral care, 'New Age' healing and the helping professions to become politically informed activities that seek personal health through social justice and social amelioration. Individual mental health can only be established through socially embedded structures that seek justice for all and not gain for the few, because individuals depend upon each other and evolve together and not in isolation. Individual dis-ease is always in part a dis-ease of society (especially when it comes down to the allocation of social resources). In this respect, a 'spirituality' that is separate from questions of social justice is a sedative for coping with an oppressive and difficult world.

In 1932 at the Alsatian Pastoral Conference at Strasbourg, Jung (1958: 334) recognised that his patients were suffering from a lack of religious perspective. It now seems that individual suffering, lone-liness and isolation are themselves consequences of a 'capitalist' spirituality that has lost its social ethic. The full consequences of this production of spirituality are as yet unknown, but what becomes clear is that psychological spirituality hides its political allegiance to a con-sumer world. As long as spirituality operates according to the dictates of global capitalism it will continue to contribute to the breaking up of traditional communities and the undermining of older, indigenous forms of life around the world. Capitalist spirituality, however, can be overcome by consideration of the forgotten social dimensions of 'the religions', by rescuing and developing alternative models of social justice, and by contesting the corporatisation and privatisation exemplified in such contemporary forms of spirituality.

In conclusion, we have seen how the history of psychology is bound up with capitalism through the privatisation of human experi-ence. When psychology ideologically reshapes religion, it creates the possibility of a spirituality for the marketplace. In this context, it is vital, as Helen Lee (2001: 155) has argued, that 'contemporary notions of spirituality, however conceived, are not romanticised as ideal and accepted unquestionably as the way forward in the twenty-first century'. While much of the discussion in this chapter has focused upon the transformations of the inner world of western Christianity, the process of privatising religious experience has also been carried forward in relation to other traditions. Indeed, as we shall see in the next chapter, the very assimilation of Asian traditions and culture into the marketplace of religions has occurred precisely through this reorganisation of experience in the terms set by psychology.

Spirituality and the Privatisation of Asian Wisdom
Traditions
Three

'Spirituality' is a means of colonising and commodifying Asian
wisdom traditions.

There is a well-known Indian parable about five blind men and an
elephant. Never encountering such a beast before, they are each led
towards it and offered a chance to feel its contours so as to gain some
appreciation of its form. The first blind man reaches out and touches
the elephant's trunk – 'It is like a huge hose,' he says. 'I would say
it is more like a spear,' says the second blind man, grasping the
tusk. 'Not at all,' says the third blind man, this time holding one
of the elephant's legs, 'It is long, round and solid like a pillar.'
'You are all wrong' says the fourth blind man stroking one of the
elephant's ears, 'It is flat and flexible like a leaf or a fan.' 'What on
earth are you all talking about?' says the fifth blind man, holding
the elephant's tail, 'It is a small animal not dissimilar to a snake or a
piece of rope.'

The parable of the blind men and the elephant is an apt metaphor
for the partiality and selectivity of many popular 'New Age' interpretations of Asian religious traditions. Aspects of such traditions are
translated into a modern western context, but there is generally a
failure to appreciate that this is not the total picture. The result is that
the wisdom of diverse ancient civilisations becomes commodified
in order to serve the eclectic interests of 'spiritual consumers' in the
contemporary New Age marketplace of religions. This fragmentation
becomes a key part of the marketing strategy for contemporary forms
of 'spirituality'. Historically rich and complex traditions are exploited
by a selective re-packaging of the tradition, which is then sold as the
'real thing'. Western Buddhist writer Vishvapani (1994) argues, for
instance, that

[T]he extent of New Age eclecticism suggests that the particular activity a New Ager chooses to participate in is secondary to the question of what they get from it, what it does for them, how it makes them feel. . . . And market forces will define as 'New Age' whatever can be sold as such (or alternatively, whatever cannot be sold as anything else). For the consuming New Ager these phenomena offer the prospect of perpetual novelty on one's own terms. If you don't like the goods, you find another supplier. . . . Carrying this a stage further, one branch of the New Age discards counter-cultural orientations in favour of 'prosperity teachings' (money as energy, life and empowerment; poverty as self-hatred). As the Sanyassin slogan had it 'Jesus saves, Moses invests, Bhagwan spends'. This is spiritualised materialism masquerading as materialised spirituality.

TAOIST INDIVIDUALISM FOR A CONSUMER AGE

Although notoriously difficult to pin down as a phenomenon, the sociologist Paul Heelas (1996: 2) suggests that the 'New Age' can best be characterised as a form of 'Self-Spirituality':

[A] common refrain [is] that 'New Age' teachings and activities do not lend themselves to being characterised in general terms . . . Beneath much of the heterogeneity [however], there is much constancy . . . This is the language of what shall henceforth be called 'Self-Spirituality'. New Agers make the monistic assumption that the Self itself is sacred . . . True, many New Agers also emphasise the spirituality of the natural order as a whole. But the fact remains that they would also agree that the initial task is to make contact with the spirituality which lies within the person.

As we have seen in previous chapters, the emergence of the modern notion of 'spirituality' as a private, introspective experience, feeling or sentiment, has its roots in the debates between the Enlightenment and Romanticism and the location of the religious in the private sphere of individual choice. This coincided in the West with the rise of 'Man' and the emergence of the 'modern' consciousness of an atomistic and autonomous self, increasingly the key organisation principle and unit of western liberal democracies. Religion entered the marketplace of human choice and experimentation, resulting in the development of that eclectic and amorphous phenomenon known as the New Age. All of these factors have had a profound impact upon the reception of Asian religious traditions and philosophies in the western world, where they have overwhelmingly been translated into introspective and otherworldly spiritualities concerned primarily with the achievement of individual enlightenment with little in the way of a social conscience or orientation to change the world in which that individual lives.

Consider for instance the example of Stephen Russell, an alternative health therapist and 'spirituality expert' based in West Hampstead with his own website (of course) and an online 'Barefoot Doctor shop'. Russell has appeared regularly on British television and in 2001/2 had a regular column in the Observer magazine, (a supplement, one of the UK's quality Sunday newspapers), where he is described as 'The Observer's own alternative therapist'. Russell is also the author of a number of popular New Age books including Barefoot Doctor's Handbook for the Urban Warrior: A Spiritual Survival Guide (1998); Return of the Urban Warrior (2001) and Liberation: The Perfect Holistic Antidote to Stress, Depression and other Unhealthy States of Mind (2002). He is a good example of contemporary prosperity-oriented spiritualities in the west, comfortable to claim the authority of ancient Asian wisdom, while promoting a philosophy of individual self-expression and social conformism.

> The kind of healing I do is based on Taoism, which provides the most nifty spiritual guidelines I've ever come across. To spice things up I also borrow liberally from Buddhism, Hinduism, Animism, Humanism and any other ism I've spent time (and money) studying.
>
> (The Barefoot Doctor, Observer, 8 July 2001)

Russell is a highly successful author and populariser of 'Eastern spirituality' in the UK. Russell's attitude to the Asian traditions that he utilises reflects the general 'pick and mix' approach that characterises New Age orientalist approaches to Asian traditions. It also stands in a long tradition of European colonialist attitudes towards Asia. What we have here is the ultimate in the commodification of other people's cultures, available for selective appropriation, repackaging and then reselling. The author even justifies such cultural appropriation on the grounds that he has paid good money to 'purchase' such cultural rights by studying them. This attitude is not dissimilar to that of multinational drug companies, who, relying on ancient indigenous knowledge of herbs and medicinal plants, patent their own chemical versions of these plants and then sell them back to the very people from whom they relied for such expert knowledge. Unfortunately, we live in a world where cultural and community rights remain as unprotected as private and corporate rights are enforced.

The Barefoot Doctor, as Russell prefers to be known following the traditional Chinese model of the itinerant acupuncturist/herbalist, provides us with a good example of a highly individualistic reading of Taoism, tailored to the needs of the contemporary western 'Urban Warrior' looking for a quick 'holistic' fix for 'unhelpful states of mind' with a dose of hip 'alternative spirituality'. The cover of one of Russell's more recent books, Liberation (2002), explicitly uses the cultural cachet of appealing to the authenticity of ancient Asian traditions to advertise the virtues of the author, while promoting the essentially accommodationist message that is by now so well established in the explosion of the popular 'Self-help' and personal development literature of recent decades:

> As always, Barefoot Doctor offers the full prescription: Taoist healing methods and philosophy, with an added pinch of Hinduism, Buddhism, Shamanism, Humanism and a heavy smattering of timeless Basic Commonsensism. Barefoot's remedies provide the perfect antidote to depression, deprivation, fear, loneliness, shyness, grief, grudges, and all the other unhelpful mind-states life in the postmodern urban spin-cycle throws up.

Inside, the reader is treated to a series of short chapters promising liberation from a series of 'unhelpful mind-states', including: 'fear of failure', 'feeling guilty', and 'being stuck in a duff relationship'. The wisdom of 'spiritual classics' like the Tao Te Ching become reduced to a philosophy of worldly accommodationism, tailored to reduce the stress and strain of modern urban life for relatively affluent westerners.

It would be worth our while at this point exploring what this 'Taoism' is that is being appealed to in such New Age literature.

> The Tao that can be spoken of is not the eternal Tao,
> Nameless is the Origin of Heaven and Earth,
> That which is Named is the Mother of all things.
> (from *Tao Te Ching*, ch. 1; translation from Addiss and
> Lombardo, 1993)

Even though, or perhaps because, it is a tradition that prides itself on being difficult to pin down, Taoism has been remarkably popular as a philosophical source for various forms of New Age spirituality, from deep ecologists interested in environmentalist readings of early Taoist thought, to business entrepreneurs looking for some ancient wisdom with some 'exotic cachet' to boost sales performance and endow their ethic of self-interest and competitiveness with some much-needed 'spiritual authenticity' (see Chapter Four). Taoism (pronounced 'Dow-ism') represents the oldest indigenous organised religion in China. The root text of the Taoist tradition (known as the *Tao Te Ching* or *The Classic on the Path and Its Virtue*) appear to date from around the third century BC. The basic themes within the early tradition are a return to natural simplicity (p'u) by giving up human social conventions and living a more authentic and spontaneous existence – that is to follow the Tao – the natural rhythms, patterns and paths of existence. Taoism did not become an organised religious movement until the middle of the second century AD when Chang Tao-ling founded the 'Celestial Masters' movement based upon the teachings of the early Taoist texts and established a lineage of Taoist priests to perform various social functions and ritual activities for the community. Traditionally, Taoism has always maintained close links to Chinese 'folk' or popular religion, especially in the countryside and villages. So much so that in practice it is often difficult to distinguish 'religious Taoism' from everyday peasant beliefs and practices. It also seems likely that the origins of Taoism are very ancient and relate to older Chinese shamanistic practices.

There were elements of the Taoist tradition that were hedonistic and concerned with the promotion of artistic creativity and the enjoyment of the finer things of life. The Seven Sages of the Bamboo Grove for instance deliberately rejected what they saw as the rigidity of Confucian social mores and conventions in favour of the cultivation of an inner spontaneity (tzu-jan). The sages wrote poems extolling the virtues of alcohol as a means of releasing oneself from inhibitions and stimulating the creative juices. In one famous incident, a visitor was shocked to find one of the sages walking around his home completely naked. When asked why he wore no clothes, the sage replied 'My house is my clothing, so what are you doing inside my trousers?'

For the purposes of classification one can talk of two types of Taoism – Philosophical Taoism (Tao chia) and Religious (or 'Lineage') Taoism (Tao chiao). It is important to bear in mind though that this is a later distinction made by Confucian-influenced interpreters wishing to make sense of the diversity of Taoist beliefs and practices. The dominant Taoist tradition has been that of the Celestial Masters (founded in 142 AD by Chang Tao-ling), which bases itself upon the teachings of the early Taoist texts. It was with the founding of this movement that Taoism became something approaching an organised religious movement with a lineage of Taoist priests performing various social functions and ritual activities for the community. In the popular religiosity of China the most important social function of the Taoist priesthood has been the preservation of the yin–yang balance of the universe through the performance of rituals (e.g. the important chiao festival, a ritual of cosmic renewal that takes place every sixty years). Taoist priests may also perform funeral services and exorcisms. The role of Taoism as a ritualistic, communal and festival religion is completely ignored in popular New Age books on Taoism.

One of the central preoccupations of Religious Taoism has been the attainment of immortality (hsien) and the practice of alchemy. In its outer or exoteric form (wai-tan) alchemical practices involved the transmutation of base metals into gold, but this practice also had an esoteric or inner form (nei-tan) which involves the transmutation of one's mortal body into an immortal body. The roots of many of these themes can be found in the classic texts of so-called 'Philosophical Taoism', which themselves serve as the key foundational works of Religious Taoism. Nevertheless, what the Taoist tradition means by immortality has shifted in different contexts and periods of history, ranging from the attainment of bodily immortality in one's own body, the development of a subtle adamantine-like body through meditative and dietary practices, the liberation of the *shen* (one's *yang*-soul) from its material counterpart – the *p'o* (or *yin*-soul), the attainment of an ineffable and deathless state of being (no doubt influenced by Buddhist notions of nirvana), to notions implying a loss of individuality and a merging with the rhythmic patterns of the Tao.

The cultural and philosophical subtleties of these various beliefs and practices, however, are flattened out when they are translated into western New Age circles. Elements of the traditional interests of Religious Taoism can be found however in the emphasis upon longevity practices. These are usually translated in western literature on self-help and personal development as a concern with health, a balanced diet (e.g. the Macrobiotic diet based on the yin–yang categorisation) and avoiding stress. Taoism of course has also been traditionally associated with the development of the martial arts and this dimension of the tradition is reflected to a limited extent in the various 'Tao of Sport' books (e.g. *The Tao of the Jump Shot*, see Figure 1: The Tao of publishing).

Taoist ideas, concepts and practices have been adopted, assimilated and transformed in innumerable ways in modern, western societies (Clarke, 2000). We should be aware of the baggage we bring to our understanding of traditions such as Taoism, particularly the modern western tendency to interpret religion as an essentially private phenomenon. From this perspective, Taoism becomes a spiritual philosophy for the individual with none of the trappings of a traditional organised religion. There are clearly elements within the diverse Taoist tradition that can feed into the image of Taoism as an individualistic philosophy (particularly the ideal of the Taoist hermit living in the wilderness and the mountains), but such elements can be found within most religions and such a picture is highly selective. Overall, the Taoist tradition has been overwhelmingly oriented towards the community (and ultimately the cosmic patterns of Tao as a whole) rather than the pursuit of individual self-interest, and even in its more philosophical and world-renouncing aspects appears to offer

GENERAL/PHILOSOPHY/NEW AGE
The Tao of Physics; The Tao of Jesus; The Tao of Islam; The Tao of Pooh; The Tao of Being; The Tao of Elvis

SCIENCE
The Tao of Science; DNA and the I Ching: The Tao of Life; The Tao of Immunology; The Tao of Bioenergetics

SPORT
The Tao of Sports; The Tao of Golf; The Tao of Sailing; The Tao of Coaching; The Tao of Teams; The Tao of the Jump Shot: An Eastern Approach to Life and Basketball

HEALTH AND WELL-BEING
Opening the Energy Gates of Your Body: The Tao of Energy Enhancement; The Tao of Medicine; The Tao of Health and Longevity; The Tao of Recovery; *The Tao of Cooking; The Tao of Eating; The Tao of Balanced Diet; The Tao of Healthy Eating; The Tao of Beauty; The Tao of Dying: A Guide to Caring*

PARENTING
The Tao of Motherhood; The Tao of Parenting

ART/CREATIVITY
The Tao of Architecture; The Tao of Design; The Tao of Watercolor; The Tao of Music

PERSONAL RELATIONSHIPS
The Tao of Sex, Health and Longevity; The Tao of Love and Sex; The Tao of Sexual Massage; The Tao of Love; The Tao of Sexology; The Tao of Conversation; The Tao of Relationships; The Tao of the Loving Couple; Couples and the Tao of Congruence' (*Journal of Couples Therapy*)

'PERSONAL GROWTH'/DEVELOPMENT
The Tao of Psychology; The Tao of Jung; The Tao of Womanhood; The Tao of Inner Peace; The Tao of Meditation; The Tao of Natural Breathing; The Tao of Learning; The Tao of Living on Purpose; The Tao of Cello (relaxation cassette)

SUCCESS AT WORK/BUSINESS
The Tao of Power; The Tao of Leadership (book and cassette); *The Tao of Negotation; The Tao of Organization; The Tao of Personal Leadership; The Tao of Management; The Tao of Sales; The Tao of Trading; The Tao of Spycraft; The Tao of American Law; The Tao of Programming*

INSTRUCTING OTHERS
The Tao of Teaching; Mentoring: The Tao of Giving and Receiving Wisdom; The Tao of Bow Wow: Understanding and Training Your Dog the Taoist Way

Figure 1: The Tao of publishing

a considerable challenge to modern western ideas of an autonomous and self-serving individual. According to Taoist thought, we are all bound up with each other and the rhythmic processes of change that constitute the rhythmic patterns of life – the Tao. This, however, is mostly lost in translation when we come to consider the various ways in which Taoism is utilised in contemporary New Age circles.

BUDDHIST WISDOM AND NEW AGE INDIVIDUALISM

Another Asian tradition that has been widely interpreted in western culture as individualistic in orientation is Buddhism. The term 'Buddhism' refers to a diverse set of traditions that take their primary inspiration from the teachings of Siddhartha Gautama, an Indian prince-turned-renouncer, who lived sometime around the fourth century BC. According to the story of Gautama's life, he was the son of a minor king in the Magadhi region of north-east India. At the age of 29, Gautama renounced his life of luxury and set out instead to learn from the various yogic and ascetic groups that existed at this time. These movements, known collectively as the Shramanas ('those who strive'), constituted the counter-culture of Gautama's day. Their common goal was to develop techniques of mental and physical discipline designed to break the chain of incessant rebirths that binds us all to a world of suffering, and to achieve liberation. After six years of yogic and philosophical experimentation, Gautama realised that the path to enlightenment and liberation (nirvana) from suffering was to be found not in extreme ascetic practices, nor in the hedonistic life he had led as a young prince, but rather in a middle path between all extremes. This became a key feature of Gautama's subsequent teaching. It is said that after many days meditating upon the nature of existence under a tree, Gautama attained enlightenment (bodhi) – a full understanding of the nature of reality. At this point he became known as 'Buddha' (Enlightened One). Gautama spent the next forty years teaching and explaining his insights to an increasing band of followers, founding in the process a monastic institution known as the sangha which has existed now for nearly two and a half millennia.

Today, 'Buddhism' represents one of the major civilisational/ religious traditions of the world and has spread from India across

South and East Asia, and in the twentieth century to the West. There are many forms of Buddhism, but the two major forms are known as Theravada ('doctrine of the elders') and Mahayana ('the Great Vehicle'). Buddhist thought in general is strongly influenced by its origins as a movement of counter-cultural renouncers, so there is inevitably a strong emphasis upon the monastic life, especially in traditional Theravada forms of Buddhism.

Buddhism entered the Euro-American cultural landscape as a consequence of European colonial expansion in the late eighteenth and nineteenth centuries. As such, its reception in the western world was intimately bound up with 'the desire to gain control, in all senses, over the newly acquired domains' (Clarke, 1997: 26). From the very beginning then, the transculturation of 'Buddhism' into a western context became embroiled in already existing tensions within western societies between Enlightenment rationalism and Romanticism, between science and religion and between the established Church and its critics (Almond, 1988; Lopez, 1998; King, 1999a).

Much of the New Age interest in Buddhism in the late twentieth century has focused upon the wisdom traditions of Mahayana forms of Buddhism (such as Japanese Zen) – and so it is these that we shall concentrate upon in our analysis. 'Mahayana' is an umbrella term for a wide variety of Buddhist movements and traditions coalescing around the universalisation of the ideal of the *bodhisattva* – beings who have vowed to dedicate their lives to the enlightenment of others.

> A Bodhisattva resolves: I take upon myself the burden of all suffering, I am resolved to do so, I will endure it . . . And why? At all costs I must bear the burdens of all beings . . . The whole world of living beings I must rescue, from the terrors of birth, of old age, of sickness, of death and rebirth.
>
> (*Vajradhvaja-sutra*, translation in Conze *et al.*, 1964: 131).

Trends that we now call Mahayana first appear to have emerged in India around the first century BC, that is some three hundred years after the Buddha's death. Mahayana Buddhism continued to revere the monastic life very highly but also advocated other more 'mundane' goals such as rebirth in the heavenly realm of *Sukhavati* ('The Blissful

Land' of the Buddha Amitabha) as spiritual 'carrots' on the way to full enlightenment. Indeed, as a whole, Buddhism has always been able to accommodate a variety of perspectives, orientations and personal motivations for Buddhist practice – from the disciplined monastic specialist working towards final liberation (nirvana) to the everyday householder aspiring to live a decent life and hoping for a favourable rebirth in their next life. Widespread belief in an endless cycle of rebirths has allowed Buddhists to take a 'long-term' perspective on their spiritual advancement, seeing it as a process taking many lives. There is no need then for all beings to be aspiring towards the same goal at the same time. It is only our conditioning from the Protestant Reformation that has made us think that members of a religion must all be working towards the same goal for that goal to be valued and endorsed by that tradition.

Although revering the monastic life, the Mahayana tradition allows for the possibility of attaining enlightenment while living as a layperson in mainstream society, though this is thought to be considerably more of a challenge. This teaching is illustrated rather well by an early Mahayana text known as The Teachings of Vimalakirti (Vimalakirti-nirdesa). This Buddhist scripture was composed in India sometime in the first two centuries of the Common Era and went on to become especially popular when Buddhism migrated to China and Japan, where it was seen as sanctioning an 'inner-worldly' discipline that appealed to a variety of groups within society, not least the Samurai.

The Teachings of Vimalakirti argues that wealth and involvement in worldly affairs are not necessarily impediments to the attainment of advanced stages on the path to full enlightenment. It propounds a vision of Buddhist practice that can usefully be compared with the 'worldly' spirituality offered by most New Age writers. The text does not demand a 'going forth' from the world and the taking up of a monastic life of renunciation, but instead suggests that the greatest test of advancement on the path to enlightenment is to maintain detachment from selfish cravings and attachments while living fully in the world as a householder. The monastic lifestyle is certainly not rejected (indeed it is said at one point that Vimalakirti has spent many previous lifetimes perfecting his self-restraint as a renouncer), but it is certainly implied that to hide oneself away from 'worldly distractions' in a community of renouncers is not to confront the problem of one's egocentric desires head-on. As Sizemore and Swearer (1993: 2) note in their study of traditional Buddhist ethics,

> To know the *dhamma* [Buddhist teachings], to see things truly, is to recognise the self as a conditioned, temporal entity and to reject self-indulgent cravings as harmful illusions. Thus, a non-attached orientation towards life does not require a flat renunciation of all material possessions. Rather, it specifies an attitude to be cultivated and expressed in whatever material condition one finds oneself. To be non-attached is to possess and use material things but not to be possessed or used by them. Therefore, the idea of non-attachment applies all across Buddhist society, to laymen and monk alike.

The story is set during the Buddha's lifetime and revolves around a wealthy householder and lay disciple of the Buddha by the name of Vimalakirti. The man in question is a rich householder. He frequents brothels and casinos, and appears on the face of it at least to be living the life of a rich playboy. Things, however, are not as they seem, and as the story in the scripture unfolds, it becomes clear that Vimalakirti has an extremely fine grasp of the subtleties of the Buddha's teaching, much to the evident chagrin of the Buddha's most revered monastic disciples who recount tales of their embarrassment when Vimalakirti demonstrates his superior knowledge of their master's teaching.

The philosophy espoused in The Teachings of Vimalakirti would appear to have some similarities with the position put forward in much of the contemporary popular literature on spirituality and personal development, such as Russell's Barefoot Doctor series, the works of Deepak Chopra and enormously successful New Age novels such as The Celestine Prophecy. Indeed superficial interpretations of Asian philosophical teachings have enabled such authors to claim 'authenticity' by selling their own philosophies of worldly accommodation as authorised by the ancient wisdom traditions of Asia.

Crucial to our understanding of this appropriation of such

traditions is a consideration of the process whereby such elision of worldviews takes place. In New Age circles and in traditional Buddhist thought a clear causal link is often made between the outward appearance of suffering and exploitation and one's own interiorised state of mind. Consider for instance the discussion that takes place in the first chapter of the *Teachings of Vimalakirti* concerning the existence of impurities in the world. The question is asked (in a manner reminiscent of the Christian 'problem of evil'), why the Buddha, if he is such a wonderful, powerful and compassionate being, allows his own particular Buddha-field of activity (i.e. this world) to contain defilements and impurities. Why isn't this the best of all possible worlds? The reply given is striking and classic Mahayana. Actually, this world is pure, the impurity that you see is simply in the eye of the beholder. When one's mind becomes purified, so does the world. In other words, if you see the world as horrible, unsatisfactory and difficult that is because of your own inner impurity, but the world is pure if your perception of it is pure and untainted! This reflects the general emphasis in Buddhist thought upon the role of the mind in constructing our picture of reality. The idea that the problems of the world are merely reflections of our own inner consciousness has become a central theme in popular New Age literature on spirituality and personal development in the late twentieth century. At first sight then, the classic Buddhist position would seem to dovetail extremely well with the privatisation and psychologisation of religion that we have discussed in Chapter Two. Such an individualisation of injustice and misfortune is one of the prime reasons why sociologists such as Paul Heelas have described the New Age as the quintessential 'religion of the self'. It has also been a key trope in western critiques of 'eastern mysticism'. How accurate, however, is it to read classical Buddhist thought as promoting modern western individualism?

The Buddhist position, as expressed above by Vimalakirti, for instance, sounds very similar to many New Age approaches. Consider what the Barefoot Doctor has to say on this matter:

> Freedom is found within. Your shackles are your own internal struggle
> – your angst and anguish, your worries about money, your frustrations,

your greed, your self-limiting thoughts, and your fears keep you from being free. But if you're willing to take a chance, to go out on a limb and download this text onto your inner hard-drive, you hold the key to liberation in your hand.

(Russell, 2002, back cover)

Similarly, one can usefully compare the Buddhist emphasis upon introspection with similar views espoused by Deepak Chopra. In *Ageless Body, Timeless Wisdom* (1993), Chopra outlines ten key steps to happiness. They are:

1 Listen to your body's wisdom.
2 Live in the present, for it is the only moment you have.
3 Take time to be silent, to meditate.
4 Relinquish your need for external approval.
5 When you find yourself reacting with anger or opposition to any person or circumstance, realise that you are only struggling with yourself.
6 Know that the world 'out there' reflects your reality 'in here'.
7 Shed the burden of judgement.
8 Don't contaminate your body with toxins, either food, drink, or toxic emotions.
9 Replace fear-motivated behaviour with love-motivated behaviour.
10 Understand that the physical world is just a mirror of a deeper intelligence.

Clearly some of these steps resemble, at least superficially, philosophical ideas that can be found within ancient Buddhist thought. Steps 5 and 6 in Chopra's scheme, for instance, are themes that can be found quite easily within the Buddhist tradition. Step 7 – shedding the burden of judgement – might appear quite similar to the Buddhist ideal of equanimity and detachment (upeksha), though in Chopra's case this is linked to the promotion of self-love, not extending compassion to all beings. Step 10 reflects Chopra's belief in an underlying divine consciousness pervading the universe (a form of modern Hindu Vedanta). While some Buddhists have expressed similar beliefs, the Buddhist philosophical tradition has generally rejected belief in any notion of a divine being as underlying cause of the universe (King, 1995). However, it is step 6 in Chopra's scheme that is worth reflecting upon – the realisation that the world 'out there' is really a reflection of one's inner reality – precisely because this sounds just like the Buddhist teaching of Vimalakirti that we have been considering.

There remains a crucial difference, however, between the New Age philosophies of Chopra and Russell and those of the Buddhist tradition. Unlike the New Age emphasis upon cultivating the self and individualising responsibility, in Buddhist thought the idea of an autonomous individual self (Sanskrit: *atman*) is precisely the *problem* to be overcome. One of the most distinctive features of the Buddha's teaching was his comprehensive rejection of the idea of a permanent self or soul. Rather, each being is a stream or constantly changing bundle of mental and material processes, more like flowing rivers than fixed essences. In this sense, the Buddhist diagnosis of our condition is that we are all essentially practising a 'religion of the self' – namely devotion to ourselves. It is this egocentricity that we must work upon so diligently, not only in order to realise that the idea of an independent self is in fact an illusion (and causes us to suffer), but also to open ourselves up emotionally to the suffering of others – those with whom we currently do *not* identify.

Compassion (Sanskrit: *karuna*) literally means 'suffering with' and it is only possible in Buddhist terms to empathise and feel the suffering of others once one has overcome one's sense of individual separation from others and by rooting out all forms of egoism and selfish attachment. This takes time, effort and vigilant practice of specific techniques of introspection – 'inner technologies of the self' (*adhyatma-vidya*), designed to gradually unravel our egocentric conception of the world. It is for this reason that the Buddhist tradition has so often been misread as being fundamentally individualistic in orientation – its focus is precisely to work on the *problem* of the individual self by exposing its contradictions and porous boundaries. This kind of work can only be done at the individual level through uprooting unwholesome (*akushala*) states of mind and false beliefs, but this only makes traditional Buddhist practice individualistic in its methods and starting-point, not in its goal or ultimate orientation. Thus, David Brazier (2001: 16–17) argues that

> Outside their proper context the Buddha's methods are meaningless and, in fact, just become diversions. The purposes of these practices is to make people better vessels for the important work to be done . . . A basic misunderstanding is that many people have come to see Buddhist training as no longer about bringing compassion to the whole world, and have, instead, started to see it as a means to a private and personal salvation. Enlightenment of this private kind may yield some limited personal satisfaction, but there is really little that is noble or honourable about it and if this is all that remains, then the main potential of Buddhism is dead.

The Buddhist traditions offer various methods for overcoming attachment to the individual self. One set of practices is known as the Four Sublime Abodes (*brahma-vihara*). These meditative techniques involve cultivating loving-kindness, compassion, sympathetic-joy and equanimity, and extending these 'other-directed' orientations towards all beings in the universe. In the Mahayana tradition, the eighth-century Buddhist poet Shantideva (695–743 AD) outlines a number of techniques for developing such an 'other-directed' orientation, including a meditation on the equality of myself and others, the 'exchange of self and others' and a contemplation of the likelihood that at some point in our innumerable rebirths, all beings have been our mother. The purpose of these contemplative techniques is to unravel or deconstruct the fixed boundaries of the individual self so that one might see things as they really are and live one's life for the sake of the flourishing of all beings, not just oneself. Thus, in what Paul Williams (1989: 198) has called 'one of the greatest spiritual poems of mankind', Shantideva outlines this vision of universal compassion:

> I am medicine for the sick. May I be both the doctor and their nurse, until the sickness does not recur.
>
> May I avert the pain of hunger and thirst with showers of food and drink. May I become both food and drink in the intermediate aeons of famine.

May I be an inexhaustible resource for impoverished beings. May I wait upon them with various forms of offering.

May I be a light for those in need of light. May I be a bed for those in need of rest. May I be a servant for those in need of service, for all embodied beings.

> (Shantideva, *Entering the Path of Enlightenment* III. 7–9, 18;
> translation in Crosby and Skilton, 1996: 20–1)

In the Buddhist tradition a key philosophical stance underlying this 'other-directed' stance is the notion of dependent co-origination (*pratityasamutpada*) – that is the reliance of all entities on factors outside themselves for their existence. There are no autonomous and self-established beings in classical Buddhist thought, not even an over-arching divine being in charge of the system as a whole. We all exist in a contingent web of causal processes, ultimately fuelled by our egocentric desires and ignorance of our true natures. Extreme fantasies that we are able to control the world on the one hand, or that we have no responsibility when acting within it on the other, are both rejected in the Buddha's teaching of the Middle Path. Contemporary Socially Engaged Buddhists such as the Vietnamese Zen monk Thich Nhat Hanh (1926–) interpret this notion in terms of a realisation of our 'inter-being'. For many contemporary Buddhists this doctrine also has important implications for the development of an ecological consciousness of bio-interdependence and non-violence towards other species and the environment. For others, such as Zen Buddhist David Loy (2003) and Thai Buddhist activist Sulak Sivaraksa (1933–) the Buddha's insights provide the basis for a profound critique of consumerism and neoliberal ideology: Sivaraksa (2002: 136) argues, for instance, that

> When an individual places self-interest above all and negates the relation view of 'self,' the result is greed and selfishness. Neoliberalist rhetoric deludes people and international organizations into believing that profits from multinational corporations will be fairly distributed in society and that any improvement in material conditions is an absolute gain for society. The ideology of consumption deludes people into

believing that constant acquisition of goods and power will lead to happiness.

The Buddhist tradition can only be described as a 'religion of the self' if we mean by this that its central preoccupation has been the *eradication* of one's sense of a separate and autonomous self. This is to be achieved through the practice of various 'introspective technologies' (*adhyatma-vidya*) aiming to develop insight into our true nature and cultivate a compassionate and non-violent attitude towards other beings. It is much more accurate then to describe the Buddhist path as a radical *critique* of the 'religion of self' in all its forms than as promoting a kind of individualistic spirituality. It is, if you like, more appropriate to describe Buddhism as an 'atheism' of the modern individual self. As Raymond Lee (2003: 364–5) has suggested, however, the traditional Buddhist 'deconstruction' of the individual self can still be co-opted by contemporary New Age approaches, particularly if they place an emphasis upon a 'decentred' or fragmentary self exploring the 'mobility of identity' and the pursuit of what they see as 'inner growth' and transformation in the privileged space of a cosmopolitan, consumerist culture. Lee argues that

> The metamorphosis of Buddhism in the context of late capitalism suggests a repositioning of the self in an economy of contingency and plurality. It is in such an economy that the self becomes receptive to Buddhist approaches to inner enlightenment. These approaches do not emphasise self-affirmation, but construe liberation as the deconstruction of the self, a method not antagonistic to the political economy of pastiche typifying late capitalism.
>
> (Lee, 2003: 365)

On Lee's analysis it would seem that the Buddhist emphasis upon 'decentring the self' cannot avoid being appropriated by the eclectic 'New Romanticism' of New Age philosophies. In response, one might argue that movements such as socially engaged Buddhism are precisely positioned to counter such trends. From this perspective, a truly 'decentred self' is one that is 'other-oriented'. Compassion for others and social engagement become a corollary of the deconstruction of the fixed boundaries of the individual self. This is a far cry from a 'postmodern' consumerist self, revelling in the play of multiple, fragmented identities but essentially remaining tied to the individual as a discrete, if fluid, entity.

The question of whether traditional Buddhist approaches lead to a political and socially revolutionary stance is an issue that is widely debated in a contemporary context. Whatever one's view on this question, it is clear that it is only if one purges traditional Buddhist teachings of their ethical, philosophical and transformative message that Buddhism can be presented as a philosophy centred upon the cultivation of the individual self rather than as one which seeks to 'de-centre' the ego from its role as the primary motivating principle for our actions in the world. This misrepresentation, of course, is pre-cisely what much of the popular literature on spirituality and personal development exploits. Thus, a vision of Buddhism is advanced that is compatible with the pursuit of personal self-development to the exclusion of a wider awareness of our interdependence with other beings and a concern for their well-being.

Socially Engaged Buddhists like Hanh provide a contemporary reading of traditional Buddhist ethical precepts in such a way that issues of social justice and oppression become foregrounded. Consider Hanh's interpretation of the second Buddhist precept (generosity):

> Aware of the suffering caused by exploitation, social injustice, stealing, and oppression, I vow to cultivate loving kindness and learn ways to work for the well-being of people, animals, plants, and minerals. I vow to practice generosity by sharing my time, energy, and material resources with those who are in real need. I am determined not to steal and not to possess anything that should belong to others. I will respect the property of others, but I will prevent others from profiting from human suffering or the suffering of other species on Earth.

Compare this to the Barefoot Doctor's prescription for 'liberation from oppression' (Russell, 2002: 158):

> People treat you according to what you unconsciously project from within. If you're feeling oppressed by others, someone in particular, a

group or the world in general, it is because you're oppressing yourself and projecting the resulting oppressive energy on to them. As soon as you stop oppressing yourself, others will stop oppressing or stop appearing to oppress you. When you stop oppressing yourself, no matter how oppressive the situation you may currently find yourself in, you will no longer feel oppressed by it.

After an anecdote about a survivor of Auschwitz surviving his ordeal through will-power and the recommendation of an acupressure point to liberate the spirit, Russell recommends the chanting of the following mantra:

'I am free to do whatever I choose, I have everything to gain and nothing to lose.'

What these two contemporary approaches to oppression share in common is a recognition that it is our perception of the world that requires transformation if we are to overcome suffering – precisely the message outlined in Buddhist texts like *The Teachings of Vimalakirti*. However, what is striking are the very different conceptions of the self and ethical consciousness that are drawn from this realisation. For Hanh, following traditional Mahayana Buddhist teachings, this inner transformation is a realisation of the profound interdependence of existence (what he calls our condition of 'interbeing'). This leads to the taming of our individual self-will and the promotion of a non-violent and 'other-directed' activism in the world. For Russell what we have is essentially the worship of the individual self and a confidence-building mantra about the omnipotence of one's own will-power as a means of achieving whatever our hearts desire. One interpretation leads to a spirituality of social and political activism, the other to a spirituality of social conformity and individual self-promotion. Hanh's Buddhist vision is fundamentally incompatible with an ethic of self-interest, consumerism and the world of aggressive corporate takeovers. Russell's is a rallying call for the heroic individualist of western society to 'make it happen' in a world where individual self-expression takes precedence over social justice and concern for the other. In this context the burden of responsibility for Russell always seems to rest with the individual: 'Suffering is a choice you make'

(Russell, 2002: 232). Similarly, the arising of any state of mind that is disturbed by the status quo is immediately dismissed as 'negative' and reduced to the level of an individual health problem: 'To feel dissatisfied is not usually so much to do with your situation as it is to do with having deficient spleen chi' (Russell, 2002: 180).

At one level this is an attempt by a holistic health practitioner to encourage westerners to take seriously traditional Chinese medical diagnosis as a helpful aid in their busy lives. At the social level, however, it is little more than a recipe for mind-control. The Stepford Wives here we come. Where, we might ask in such accounts, is the recognition of the value of experiencing dissatisfaction with the world and the wider social and political context of oppression? Should our reaction to outrages like Auschwitz really be to promote a philosophy of 'grin and bear it'? What we find in such works is an extreme individualisation of suffering and oppression (it is always your problem, deal with yourself, not with society) and the constant assertion of the power and freedom of the individual self to recreate the reality that they encounter. It is 'feel good' spirituality for the urban and the affluent and it has nothing to say to the poor and the marginalised in society, other than offering them a regime of compliance, a new 'opiate for the masses'.

According to the UN report on Human Development for 1999 1.3 billion people survive on less that one US dollar a day and whereas the richest 20% of the world's population enjoy 86% of its consumption, the poorest 20% consume only 1.3%. Between 1960 and 1989, the gulf between rich and poor nations has doubled. The gulf between the rich and the poor in general continued to increase throughout the 1990s. However, in the carefree and affluent worlds of writers like Russell and Chopra such statistics have no bearing or impact. There is no mention of dealing with poverty, social injustice or inequality, except insofar as these are seen as a condition of the modern individual's own self-imposed oppression and limitation. These forms of spirituality, despite their avant-garde appeal to those who would see themselves as counter-cultural and free from the traditional forms of social control associated with the mainstream religions, provide new psychologised technologies for promoting social conformism, all the more disturbing for their claims to be 'hip' and 'alternative'.

This trend has led some to claim that 'eastern spirituality' can only be distorted by its transplantation to a western cultural context. Indeed since Albert Schweitzer and Max Weber it has been a constant theme within western accounts of Asian traditions to suggest that when imported to the West their philosophies are at worst amoral and at best lacking in the necessary ethical foundations to combat social injustice. As Harvey Cox (1977: 84) has suggested:

> The problem is, however, that in a culture like ours, already steeped in the philosophy of 'You do your thing and I'll do mine,' the lofty Buddhist idea of nonattachment can hardly escape distortion. Westerners will not be able to practice the Oriental posture of nonattachment until they move not just beyond attachments but also beyond an 'I' which does 'my thing'. Real nonattachment will become possible only when self slips away too. But this is something most Westerners either cannot or will not concede.

By implication such claims are always made by negatively contrasting such traditions to western Christianity and/or various 'secular' worldviews, even if this comparison is often implicit. Such orientalist accounts generally presuppose that internally diverse traditions such as 'Buddhism', 'Hinduism' and 'Taoism' can only be read one way. Clearly the examples of militaristic (Samurai) and socially engaged interpretations of Zen Buddhism demonstrate that this is not the case, nor has it ever been.

Spirituality as a Challenge to the Status Quo

Both New Age accommodationist 'religions of the self' and Hanh's Socially Engaged Buddhism are of course modern responses to the challenge of developing a 'spirituality' that engages with the contemporary world (King and Queen, 1996; Queen 2000). Within the academic and Buddhist communities there is a lively debate about the extent to which contemporary Socially Engaged Buddhism reflects traditional Buddhist teachings or is essentially a modern innovation (see Yarnall, 2003). Similar debates have occurred with regard to the emergence of Liberation Theology within Latin American Christianity and Dalit Theology among the 'Untouchable' communities of India.

There is of course no call for social revolution in the Buddhist *Teaching of Vimalakirti* – at least not in the *modern* (i.e. post-Enlightenment) sense of a radical social, economic and political reconfiguration of social structures as a whole. This should not surprise us since the text was composed in a very different milieu and at a time when 'social revolution' and mass mobilisation in the modern sense were not considered viable possibilities. What is remarkable about the *Teachings of Vimalakirti* however is that it *does not* take the philosophy of 'impurity exists in the eye of the beholder' as an endorsement of the status quo. There is no individualist accommodation to the prevailing social conditions and attitudes, nor do we find an 'easy' path to spiritual fulfilment advocated. There may be no call for mass mobilisation and political revolution in the sense of say the French Revolution of 1789 or the overthrow of Communism in Eastern Europe in 1989, but this is a reason for us to be cautious about evaluating such ancient texts according to our own ethnocentric and anachronistic standards rather than for condemning the text for failing to provide modern solutions to social injustice. Nevertheless, in a fashion that in its own context was *revolutionary* for a sacred text of its time, Vimalakirti proceeds to challenge the taken-for-granted social relations, hierarchies and authority figures of his day. Revered Buddhist monks are ridiculed for their limited understanding of the Buddha's message, and *bodhisattvas* (spiritually advanced beings well on the path to full enlightenment) are reproached for failing to grasp the transformative and universalist nature of the Buddha's teachings.

The central motif in the story of Vimalakirti surrounds his illness. As the story unfolds it becomes clear that Vimalakirti has not left his home for some time because of his illness. This serves as the spur for the Buddha to asks a veritable coterie of traditional Buddhist 'celebrities' – his most famous monastic disciples and other spiritually advanced beings (known as *bodhisattvas*) if they will visit Vimalakirti to enquire as to his state of health. Each figure, together amounting to the most revered and authoritative figures within the Buddhist tradition as a whole, declines the invitation and proceeds to recount tales of the layman Vimalakirti embarrassing them with his superior grasp of the Buddha's teachings.

Shariputra, the primary exemplar of wisdom (*prajna*) in the early Buddhist tradition, and one of the most senior monastic figures in the Buddha's retinue, declines to visit Vimalakirti because on a previous encounter the layman instructed him to realise that meditative contemplation is best practised while being fully involved in the world, rather than seeing it as a solitary practice to be carried out in monastic isolation. Later on, this same Shariputra encounters a goddess and, being impressed by her subtle grasp of the Buddha's teaching, asks her, in classic male-chauvinist fashion, why, if she is such a wise and powerful goddess, she does not transform her body into that of a male to improve her prospects of enlightenment. The goddess replies that for twelve years she has searched for the specific qualities of femaleness and has failed to find any. From what then will she change? At that point the goddess changes places with Shariputra, temporarily making him appear as a goddess and herself as the male monk Shariputra. The goddess then explains that the Buddha's teaching knows no distinction between male and female. So much for male chauvinism! Elsewhere in the text Vimalakirti reproaches a young noble who wishes to honour him with a necklace of precious jewels. Why would I need these, Vimalakirti declares, give them to the poor instead where they will be of some use:

> The giver who makes gifts to the lowliest poor of the city, considering them as worthy of offering as the [Buddha] himself, the giver who gives without any discrimination, impartially, with no expectation of reward, and with great love – this giver, I say, totally fulfills the Dharma-sacrifice.
>
> (Thurman, 1991: 41)

Even Maitreya, revered by all Buddhists as the next Buddha, is embarrassed by Vimalakirti when he is told that he should not consider himself to be particularly special since enlightenment is for everyone. Eventually, it transpires that Vimalakirti's illness is the result of his advanced stage on the path to enlightenment and is a physical manifestation of his refusal to distinguish his own sense of self-existence from that of all other beings in the universe. Vimalakirti declares that he is ill precisely because he feels the illness (dukkha) of all other beings – experiencing what Mahayana Buddhists call 'the great compassion' (maha-karuna):

> my sickness . . . will last as long as do the sicknesses of all living beings. Were all living beings to be free from sickness, I also would not be sick . . . Thus, recognizing in his own suffering the infinite sufferings of these living beings, the bodhisattva correctly contemplates these living beings and resolves to cure all sicknesses.
>
> (Thurman, 1991: 43, 45)

Of course, we need to keep in mind the specific historical and cultural location of the text. As a sacred text expounding Buddhist teachings and ideals, the story of Vimalakirti is hagiography in the classical Indian style of hyperbole. However, what stands out in a comparison between the Teachings of Vimalakirti and many contemporary popular works on spirituality and personal development is that the Buddhist text, despite its considerable antiquity, offers an intellectual, moral and transformative challenge to social norms, while New Age writers like Russell and Chopra provide little more than techniques for overcoming anxiety and conforming to existing social norms.

Consider for instance the Barefoot Doctor's prescription for liberation from wanting. How does the author relate to the sickness of his own contemporary consumer society – that is the incessant desire to acquire more and more things? Here is a perfect opportunity for Russell to provide some critical distance from the rampant con- sumerism of his day. The book states that one has three options: enter a monastery and contemplate the rise and fall of your desires until you achieve nirvana (an option it presents to the reader as arduous and impractical), spend the rest of your life trying to acquire the things that you want, or third (the option that the book promotes), a combination of the two. Russell (2002: 118–9) continues:

> do what you can to get what you want, while watching from within the internal dialogue that goes on incessantly about what, who, where and how you want what you want and what it feels like once you've got it,

while reminding yourself that it's all theatre, and behind all the
longing, for no matter what or whom, is the longing to be home, to be at
peace with yourself.

Like the figure of Vimalakirti, contemporary New Age 'gurus' like the
Barefoot Doctor, and others we shall discuss in Chapter Four such as
Deepak Chopra and Osho/Bhagwan Shree Rajneesh, place tremendous
emphasis upon a spirituality while 'living in the world' as opposed to
the more traditional approach which involves the adoption of a
monastic life of renunciation. However, what made the *Teachings of
Vimalakirti* so *revolutionary* in its time was that the kind of 'inner-worldly
spirituality' that it advocates constituted a *social* challenge to the
accepted social ideals and institutional authorities of its time. What
must revered members of the Buddhist monastic community (*sangha*)
have made of this text, which not only pokes fun at their pretensions
to superior wisdom, but also lampoons their most authoritative
monastic figures? The text challenges the conventionally accepted
dichotomies, authority structures and assumptions of its day (most
notably ideas about the superiority of males, the monastic life, and
donating to the *sangha* instead of giving to the poor). The text also
'raises the bar' of spiritual conduct by arguing that the conquering of
selfish desires and the achievement of true detachment can best be
demonstrated and tested by living fully within the world and con-
fronting one's desires. Such a claim is as subversive a perspective as
you are likely to find within the context of a traditional Buddhist
society that revered the monastic community as the supreme moral
and spiritual authority of the day and viewed spiritual progress in
terms of renunciation from the world. Of the modern spiritual
teachers who make similar intellectual moves it is perhaps Osho
Rajneesh who comes closest to this level of iconoclasm in a contemporary context. We should be clear, however, that there is no talk
of social justice or helping the poor in Rajneesh, just the promise of
individual enlightenment. The worldly spiritual path of the Buddhist
example of Vimalakirti is only possible because of the innumerable
lives of intense renunciation that he is said to have performed, perfecting the virtues of patience and compassion, etc. This stands in

sharp contrast to the relatively 'easy' attainment of enlightenment promised by figures such as Osho and Deepak Chopra, which seems to require little in the way of preliminary disciplines of self-denial and shows much less interest in becoming 'other-oriented' (see Chapter Four). As Chopra suggests in his bestselling book *Ageless Body, Timeless Mind* (1993: 258): 'Don't struggle against the infinite scheme of things, instead be at one with it.'

At the more popular end of the spectrum we have New Age writers like Chopra and the Barefoot Doctor telling us to do what we want, albeit with the occasional recommendation that we should reflect upon whether we really want all of these things. 'This-worldly-ism' is the mainstream ideology of our times. In a modern secular and capitalist society it is not counter-cultural or subversive to promote spiritual practices that involve conforming to a consumerist lifestyle of self-indulgence, individualism and 'inner-worldliness'. The Barefoot Doctor's prescription for our problems, for instance, involves little more than an accommodation of the individual to the rampant consumerism of our day:

> Competitiveness is what fuels evolution, let alone a free market economy. And it would be misguided to see it as a Western disease. Having trained for 30-odd years in Chinese martial arts, I can tell you that no one is as competitive as the Orientals. The difference is that they, under the influence of Taoism and Buddhism, learned to use their competitive energy with the things that count. Hence it would be unlikely to find three Triad members seeing who can last the longest in the sauna in Gerrard Street. They'd rather use the energy to see who can win the most money at cards after they've showered off.
>
> (The Barefoot Doctor, column in the *Observer*,
> 10 February 2002)

The figure of Vimalakirti is meant to exemplify the Mahayana Buddhist idea that liberation (nirvana) is to be found within the world (*samsara*), rather than by an escape from it. It is perfectly legitimate within the Buddhist tradition to interpret nirvana as a transformative wisdom about the true nature of this world rather than as the realisation of some distant and otherworldly goal beyond the universe. 'Buddha,' after all, means 'one who has awakened'. Spiritual transcendence in these terms is nothing more than being fully immanent in the here and now. *Be here now*. To be enlightened then is to see things as they really are – to wake up. This is a 'spiritual' transformation, but not one that involves leaving or transcending the world, only seeing it for what it is and changing one's behaviour and orientation accordingly. The everyday world does not disappear upon enlightenment (just as the Buddha did not disappear in a puff of smoke when he achieved enlightenment), but one could say that the universe becomes illuminated or seen in a new way by our newly transformed perspective upon it. However, we do not 'go' anywhere. Nirvana means the 'blowing out' of the flames of our selfish desires. When asked where does an enlightened being go after his death the Buddha replied, 'Do you ask where a fire goes when the flame goes out?'

Many of the New Age authors who appeal to Asian wisdom traditions are right to challenge traditional 'other-worldly' stereotypes of traditions such as Buddhism and Taoism, as the example of the worldly Buddhist 'saint' Vimalakirti and a detailed analysis of Taoist philosophy and history demonstrate rather well. We are being misled however when they interpret such teachings as implying an *accommodation* to one's individualistic desires and the world as it is. *Buddhist teachings aim at undercutting our individual 'religions of the self' by deconstructing the 'self' that is the object of our devotion.* By contrast, the kind of New Age teachings that we commonly find sold to us as 'Asian spirituality' reflect a very western cultural *obsession* with the individual self and a distinct lack of interest in compassion, the disciplining of desire, selfless service to others and questions of social justice.

YOGA AND THE WEST: FALLING INTO THE CARTESIAN TRAP

A similar translation process has occurred with the popular development of Hindu-based yoga practices in the West, transforming yoga from a set of renunciatory practices for attaining liberation from the cycle of rebirths either into a psychologised 'spirituality of the self' on the one hand or into a secularised system of therapy, physical exercise and/or mood-enhancement on the other.

Yoga, according to the Hindu classic the *Yoga Sutra* (fourth century AD) can be defined as that which leads to 'the cessation of mental fluctuations' (*Yoga Sutra* 1.2). These fluctuations (*vritti*) comprise all of our mental functions, from perceptual experiences to reasoned arguments, errors of knowledge to dreams, deep sleep and our memories (*Yoga Sutra* 1.6). It is these everyday states of consciousness, characterised as they are by constant fluctuation or 'alteration', that cause suffering and therefore require calming according to Patanjali, author of the *Yoga Sutra*. Rather than promoting the cultivation of 'altered states of consciousness' then as it is often represented in western psychological accounts, the goal of classical yoga (known as 'Royal' – *raja* – yoga) is precisely to *prevent* such states from arising by the promotion of a state of lasting inner contentment and stability of mind. The way to pacify our fluctuating mental states is by eradicating selfish desires through the vigilant practice of yogic techniques (*Yoga Sutra* 1.12). This relates to the 'eight limbs' (*asta-anga*) of classical yoga. They are:

1 Ethical discipline (self-control in relation to the outer world)
2 Self-discipline (inner control)
3 Posture
4 Practice of breath-control
5 Withdrawal of the senses (the internalisation of consciousness)
6 Practice of concentration
7 Attainment of meditative absorption
8 Unitive awareness (*samadhi*)

Eventually, the yoga practitioner is said to be able to reverse the outward flow of consciousness, making it introspective (*Yoga Sutra* 1.29) and reflexive. The yogin is then in a position to distinguish between the true self – the pure and transcendent consciousness that witnesses all that we experience through our many lives – from the fluctuating experiences of our mind and body that we conventionally think of as our 'self'.

Classical Hindu yoga, then, like the various Buddhist 'inner technologies of the self', is fundamentally concerned with overcoming our misconceptions about the nature of the self and the egocentric impulses that this ignorance feeds. However, whereas Buddhist philosophy rejects the idea of a permanent self completely, the Hindu traditions generally postulate a kind of unchanging and permanent essential self (*atman* or *purusa*) underlying the flux of experiences we have as individually embodied beings (for a fuller discussion of these differences see King, 1999b). Nevertheless, what both of these Indian-derived 'spiritualities' share in common is a comprehensive and radical critique of the conventional ego-driven and particularised self that sees itself as the all-important focus of our lives – as the centre of our universes. This challenge to our everyday understanding of the self and its desires is lost however when yoga is transformed in modern western societies into an individualised spirituality of the self, or, as we are increasingly seeing, repackaged as a cultural commodity to be sold to the 'spiritual consumer'.

The initial reception of Hindu yoga in the West was highly intellectualised and was influenced by the missionary activities of Swami Vivekananda and the work of western orientalist scholars. As we saw in Chapter One, Vivekananda has been crucial in the planting of the idea that Indian religions – Hinduism in particular – constitute the home of spirituality. In his lectures and promotion of yoga throughout Europe and North America in the late nineteenth and early twentieth centuries, as well as in the orientalist scholarship of the time, the emphasis was very much upon the philosophical dimensions of yoga, rather than its practice, or social or institutional dimensions. For Vivekananda the form of yoga he promoted (known as *Jnana yoga* or the yoga of knowledge) constituted a kind of 'Applied Psychology' that could be usefully adapted for the western world. Thus, the mainstream reception of yoga (and by implication all Asian meditative systems) into the western imaginaire was from the beginning translated into the emerging discourse of psychology. This has had profound implications in the West, with Asian traditions being portrayed as 'mystical', experiential and individualistic in nature.

The history of yoga practice in South Asia is a mixture of many different traditions, practices and worldviews. Like the Buddhist and Taoist examples we have considered, Hindu forms of yoga involve the prolonged application of 'psychosomatic' techniques designed to undermine egocentricity, discipline desire and transform one's perspective upon reality. However, what we call psychology (the systematic study of the self) and cosmology (our worldview or conception of the universe) were not distinguished in the various yoga traditions of South Asia. One of the problems with the psychologisation of yoga then is that it erases the cultural context and institutional setting of such practices. At first, some might see this as a positive step in the emergence of a more universal spirituality – by detaching yoga practices from the culturally specific belief-systems of Asia they can be universalised for a global context. However, yoga is not left in a 'free floating' and decontextualised state by this move, as if western psychology were a culturally neutral discourse without its own metaphysical context and value-system. Rather yoga becomes *recoded* in the terms of modern psychological discourse and the individualist values of the western society from which that mindset originates. In this way yoga loses much of what is genuinely counter-cultural, transformative and challenging to western cultural norms. It becomes secularised, de-traditionalised and oriented exclusively towards the individual. Thus, as Kimberley Lau notes (2000: 96, 112)

> As first commodified and subsequently practiced in the United States and many other countries in the world, yoga and t'ai chi are removed from their philosophical contexts and largely undertaken as physical exercise regimens, though still presented within the context of body–mind integration and spirituality. In essence, the physical elements of the philosophical systems have come to represent – and be – what we call yoga and t'ai chi, . . . thereby largely separating the two practices from their respective belief systems that rely on physical movements as only one aspect of a complete practice.

The widespread popularity of yoga in the West is largely linked to its secularisation (that is the separation of the practice of yoga from its religio-philosophical rationale). This secularisation process began initially in India in the late 1930s when a number of yoga teachers sought to adapt traditional yoga practices for the general public. One figure in particular, however, stands out in the transformation of yoga into a popular practice in the West and that is B. K. S. Iyengar. Iyengar taught a form of postural yoga, based upon the traditional practices of Hatha Yoga ('the yoga of force') and largely through his connection with the violinist Yehudi Menuhin, developed an international reputation as a yoga teacher. Hatha yoga is a more physical-based system of yoga practice than classical yoga, and aims to achieve enlightenment through the transformation of one's body. As such, it places much emphasis upon one of the traditional 'eight limbs' of classical yoga – namely posture (*asana*) as a means of awakening one's 'consciousness that is coiled up like a snake' (*kundalini*) through the various 'power centres' (*chakras*) of the body, until one reaches a state of full-awakening. Iyengar, however, downplays the religio-philosophical dimensions of such practices, in favour of their more physical aspects. Generally speaking, popular yoga practice in the West has emphasised physical postures and perhaps breath-control techniques, but tends to ignore the ethical and ascetic dimensions of yoga practice. Similarly, there is much less emphasis, if any, upon the explicit goal of such yoga systems, which is the realisation of a state of heightened and internalised awareness that transforms one's conception of the self and of the universe as a whole. With the secularisation of yoga almost complete, Iyengar has been instrumental in the cultural reception of yoga in the West as a physical regime designed to promote relaxation, exercise and good health (for a discussion of the western reception of yoga see Michelis, 2004).

The domestication of yoga can be seen in the two ways in which it has been represented in the West – as a bodily regime (largely influenced by Iyengar's popularisation of Hatha Yoga practice in the West) or as a discipline for mood-enhancement, stress-relief and (for those who prefer more spiritual sugar in their coffee), the cultivation of blissful altered states of consciousness (as in, Maharishi Mahesh Yogi's *Transcendental Meditation* and Swami Sivananda's *Divine Life Society*). Despite the frequent appeals to a 'holistic' approach, the popular reception of yoga in the West has largely fallen into a Cartesian trap of emphasising either the mind or the body. Both the intellectualist/ psychological reading of yoga among the humanist and transpersonal psychologists on the one hand, and the more widespread physicalist approaches of traditions like Iyengar's on the other, provide partial accounts of the significance of yoga systems of practice. The first, emphasising the mind, privatises yoga, making it a practice for the individual attainment of certain extraordinary psychological states of consciousness. This trend, initially introduced into the West by Vivekananda at the turn of the twentieth century, really took off in the West during the counter-cultural revolutions of the late 1960s, where yoga became linked to the emerging experimental drug culture and a generational critique of the mainstream values of post-war western societies. The second way in which yoga has been popularised in the West often used the 'exoticism' of the first trend as its public platform, but emphasised the body rather than the mind. Yoga essentially became a form of exercise and stress-relief to be classified alongside the other health and 'sports-related' practices and fads of the late twentieth century.

Today it is largely the more physicalist aspects emphasised by Iyengar that dominate the 'yoga market' in the West. The earlier psychologisation of yoga in the West remains a key approach among the bourgeois world of so-called 'counter-cultural' or 'alternative' spir-

> 'Less Inner Thigh, More Inner Peace: Our Yoga Workout Will Give you Lean, Sexy Legs and a Shot of Serenity, Too. Om, Sweet Om!'
>
> Title of article by Suzanna Markstein in *Mademoiselle* magazine, June 1999, see Lau, 2000: 123.

itualities that first emerged among the educated middle classes in the late 1960s. The contemporary marketing of yoga of whatever type, however, often appeals to the exoticism and 'counter-cultural cachet' of yoga as a key selling-point – except in those cases where to appear too 'mystical', 'religious' or 'ethnic' might put off customers looking for some light relief from the stresses of their busy urban lives. Again, we should stress that we do not wish to dismiss the potential health benefits of certain yoga practices, or make the claim that there is no possibility for 'authentic' yoga practice in the West. Overall, however, it is clear that the metaphysical, institutional and societal dimensions of ancient yoga traditions are largely lost in the translation and popularisation of yoga in the West. Ancient techniques of introspection and self-control designed to transform one's orientation *away* from a false identification with the individual self and leading to a deep confrontation with one's existential condition, become instead optional methods for relieving daily stress and allowing individuals to cope better with the stresses and strains of the modern capitalist world. An arduous path to enlightenment and liberation from the cycle of rebirths through the conquest of selfish desires becomes yet another modern method for pacifying and accommodating individuals to the world in which they find themselves.

CONCLUSION

The renunciatory spiritualities of Asia, such as Hindu yoga, the various Buddhist traditions and early Taoist philosophy, far from providing sustenance for a philosophy of accommodation to contemporary consumerism and atomistic individualism, furnish us instead with ancient 'inner technologies' and philosophies for overcoming the destructive cycle of cravings that we valorise today as 'consumerism'. In the place of egocentric and worldly desires such traditions seek to develop 'other-directed' ethical ideals such as compassion and consideration for others by dissolving the fantasies of an autonomous individual self at the centre of our world. In Mahayana Buddhism, for instance, this is exemplified by the goal of the *bodhisattva*, who remains in the world, having realised its emptiness, and attaining enlightenment in order to work for the enlightenment or 'consciousness-raising' of others who have yet to achieve such a realisation. The 'perfect wisdom' of the enlightened being, however, involves a profound displacement and challenge to conventional perceptions of the world and of the self. It is a 'revolution of the foundations' (*ashraya-paravritti*) of our everyday experiences rather than a confirmation of them. Moreover, in the realisation of such higher wisdom, the conventional search for individual desire-fulfilment and daily comforts is completely subverted as we increasingly come to realise the interdependence of all beings. Such a goal involves the eradication of any notion of a separate individual ego as the motivating force behind one's actions. The notion of the autonomous self-serving individual is a myth. The purpose of life, as the Dalai Lama has stated on a number of occasions, is to live for the sake of others – as exemplified in the twin ideals of Buddhism – wisdom and compassion.

In the Hindu yoga traditions the goal is to overcome selfish attachments through the practice of a rigorous regime of psycho-physical techniques designed to turn the consciousness of the practitioner inward. This process, however, is designed not to reinforce one's sense of an individual embodied self but to overcome it. Depending upon the specific yoga tradition this can mean anything from identifying with a transcendent consciousness beyond the material world (classical Raja Yoga), realising the essential unity of existence (Advaita Vedanta), or identifying with the Supreme Deity or seeing the entire universe as one's body (various forms of Tantra). Whatever their fundamental worldview, all forms of Hindu yoga reject the motivational structure upon which consumerism is predicated – namely identification with the embodied individual self and acting to further its own self-interest.

In Chinese 'spiritual classics' such as the *Tao Te Ching*, the sage advocates a life of profound simplicity with no need for acquisitiveness or competition with others (*Tao Te Ching*, ch. 81). One can offer a political reading of the text, as some ancient Chinese commentators did, but it is not easily reconciled with a modern consumerist or capitalist ideology. If anything the philosophy of early Taoism seems to have more in common with E. H. Schumacher's philosophy of 'Small is Beautiful'. The Taoist ideal of the uncarved block (*p'u*) involves overcoming the inauthentic desires and aspirations that mainstream society drums into us by returning to a condition of childlike, natural spontaneity (*tzu-jan*).

These classic Asian texts and traditions, although philosophically quite distinct from each other and capable of diverse readings on many different issues, remain fundamentally concerned with transforming one's perspective on life. This involves a reorientation *away* from the concerns of the individual and towards an appreciation of the wider social and cosmic dimensions of our existence. These Asian traditions can be more easily read today as profound critiques of consumerism and a 'spirituality of self' rather than as an endorsement of them. Much of the contemporary literature on 'spirituality', rather than picking up the richness and complexity of Asian wisdom traditions, privatises them for a western society that is oriented towards the individual as *consumer* and society as *market*. As we shall see in the next chapter, this cultural translation opens up the space for the corporate takeover of religion.

Four

Spirituality has become the primary means facilitating the corporate takeover of religion.

By the time they are seven, the average American child will be seeing 20,000 advertisements a year on television. By the time they are 12 they will have an entry in the massive marketing databases used by companies.
David Boyle, *The Tyranny of Numbers*, 2001, p. 91

The silent takeover of religion has few ethical limits. Indeed, by the beginning of the twenty-first century the selling of souls has gone online. In 2001, Adam Burtle of Woodinville, Washington, placed an advertisement on eBay, the online auction house. The advert read:

> 20 yr old Seattle boy's SOUL, hardly used . . . Please realise, I make no warranties as to the condition of the soul. As of now, it is near mint condition, with only minor scratches.

The advert was eventually withdrawn by eBay auctioneers, insisting that auctioned items must be merchandise that can physically change hands, but not before a bid of $400 had been made and Burtle's soul was sold to a woman in the Midwest. A year later 24-year-old Nathan Wright from West Des Moines also placed his soul up for auction on eBay, and then when this was also forcibly withdrawn, on Yahoo. Eventually Wright's soul was sold to a television sound mixer in Los Angeles for $31 plus $15 dollars for shipping and handling (Wright sent his soul in a jar that he said 'may or may not' have contained fudge in it at some time.)

How is one to interpret such acts? Placing the ad can obviously be seen as a joke, and, as in the case of Wright at least, a publicity stunt for his own web-based magazine. The completion of the transaction by a buyer, however, and the exchange of money implies an element of parody and transgression. Certainly, the decision by eBay officials to pull such adverts suggests that the company sees such acts as subversive of its business rationale, since it problematises the materialistic logic underlying the system of exchange. For his part, Wright did not see why eBay should object, 'It's in a glass jar. It's a tangible object,' he said. 'Besides, they're getting buyer's fees, so I don't see the problem.' Humorous though this story is, the account Wright gives of his entrepreneurial idea is also suggestive of the effects upon desire and behaviour of the potential commodification of *everything* in a late capitalist context – that is the transformation of humans into consumers, addicted to the desiring effects of buying and selling:

> It all started when I was selling normal stuff like a computer monitor and a mouse . . . But eBay is kind of addictive. You start listing one thing and then you look around your house and say, 'Well, what else could I sell?'
>
> (Nathan Wright, *The Des Moines Register*, 20 May 2002)

The commodification, packaging and selling of one's soul in the twenty-first century is indicative of another feature of contemporary society, viz., the increasing hegemony of a narrowly instrumental and calculative rationality as the basis for all truth-claims and value judgements. From this perspective if its value cannot be quantified then it cannot be valuable! The desire to quantify something and neatly calculate is the ethos of a neoliberal philosophy where everything can be shaped in terms of the market. Although the idea of selling one's 'soul' was in part a marketing joke, putting the idea of selling the 'soul' into a commercial framework illustrates the emerging values of capitalist spirituality very well. The very intangibility of a metaphysical reality – an idea or belief – is packaged and marketed by appealing to an existing cultural narrative about the idea of selling the soul. The Faustian dilemma takes on a new dimension of novelty in a consumerist context.

> FAUST: And soothe my soul to self-sufficiency,
> And make me one of pleasure's devotees,

Then take my soul, for I desire to die:

And that's a wager!

MEPHISTOPHELES: Done!

FAUST: And done again!

If to the fleeting hour I say

'Remain, so fair thou art, remain!'

Then bind me with your fatal chain,

For I will perish in that day.

(Johann Wolfgang Von Goethe, *Faust: Part One*,

Penguin, 1986, p. 87)

In a culture characterised by an addiction to buying and selling, 'spirituality' has, as we noted earlier, become the brand name for the act of selling off the assets of 'old time' religion. Religious artefacts and language have 'cachet value' for a society of isolated individuals, hungry for packaged meaning. They provide a nostalgic sense of an imagined religious past where the universe was meaningful, people were devout and life made sense according to the values of one's community or group. 'Spiritual capital' works by distancing itself from religious institutions and 'incorporating' them into the market. The situation has now come full circle. Recognising its depleting numbers in a consumer society, the Christian church (particularly right-wing evangelical groups) now seeks to win people over to Sunday service through the power of advertising. One advertising agent in the UK, when asked if there was any difference between selling baked beans and boosting church attendance, replied clearly in the negative (*Today Programme*, BBC Radio 4, 14 August 2003). Whether or not there is value in such processes in recruiting new members into the Church, it reflects the increasing attempt to direct people's desires through aggressive marketing techniques. The explicit use of marketing to boost one's product image entered the public sphere of UK politics in the 1980s when the PR company Saatchi and Saatchi was engaged by Mrs Thatcher to boost the electoral fortunes of the Conservative Party. It is now an established feature of politics on both sides of the Atlantic, with President George W. Bush employing the marketing expertise of Charlotte Beers, who made her name selling Uncle Ben's

Rice and Head and Shoulders shampoo, to 'rebrand America' after 9/11.

The adoption of vigorous marketing techniques in politics has, as Naomi Klein (2002: 186-7, 188) suggests, potentially dangerous consequences for democratic politics:

> 'From a marketing point of view, you don't introduce new products in August.'
> White House Chief of Staff Andrew H. Card, Jr, on selling the 'War on Iraq' to the American people, cited in the *New York Times*, 7 September 2002.
>
> 'In any great brand, the leverageable asset is the emotional underpinning of the brand.'
> Charlotte Beers on 'rebranding America', cited in Peter Carlson, 'The U.S.A. Account' *Washington Post*, 31 December 2001.

> In the corporate world, once a 'brand identity' is settled on by head office, it is enforced with military precision throughout a company's operations . . . At its core, branding is about rigorously controlled one-way messages, sent out in their glossiest form, then hermetically sealed off from those who would turn corporate monologue into social dialogue . . . When companies try to implement global image consistency, they look like generic franchises. But when governments do the same they can look distinctly authoritarian.

One of the effects of embracing consumerism in the Christian tradition has been that it has become easier to view attendance at church as a lifestyle commodity rather than as an ethical response. In its attempt to appear relevant the Christian Church can easily conform to corporate images and utilise its language, without examining the political problems of how such companies or knowledge might be linked to global issues of debt or poverty. This kind of marketing of Christianity, especially in the USA, is nothing new, having roots that go back at least to the emergence of prosperity religions in the nineteenth century. A religion of feel-good affluence reassures the consuming public that religion can indeed be just another feature of the capitalist world with little or no social challenge to offer to the world of business deals and corporate takeovers. Spirituality is appropriated for the market instead of offering a countervailing social force to the ethos and values of the business world. This is not to assume that we can ever escape the influence of the market, but rather to recognise that the utilisation of a 'spirituality' tailored for business enterprise ignores vital aspects of those traditions upon which it relies – aspects that directly challenge the privatisation and commercialisation of life.

CAPITALIST SPIRITUALITY AND BUSINESS-ETHICS: AN IMPORTANT DISTINCTION

In this chapter we want to draw attention to a difference between a 'business ethics' approach and capitalist spirituality by highlighting how the corporate takeover of religions uses the idea of 'spirituality' as a support for its own values. It is important to reiterate at this point that we are not arguing for an 'accurate' or 'true' use of the word 'spirituality' but rather against the predominant usage in the business world which selectively uses religious traditions as resources for marketing its own ideological values. Business interests override the social value of the traditions, showing that, in many ways, the new god is 'capital' itself.

The relationship between business and religion is a complex one. In the introduction we set out our typology of 'spiritual movements' in terms of their accommodation to capitalism and noted the rise of capitalist spirituality, which uncritically subordinates spiritual/religious concerns to an overriding business-orientation. It is important at this point to make a distinction, between

businesses that seek to use 'ethical' values in their practice

and

the marketing of 'spirituality' within business as a form of product-enhancement

In the first case ethical considerations derived from social traditions 'outside the market' inform business activities and act as a countervailing corrective to exploitation, offering an appreciation of the wider dimensions of life. In this regard, it is clear that there is a role for the ethical systems within, for example, Christianity, Judaism, Islam, Buddhism and Hinduism to play within the business world. This relates to the reformist position within our fourfold typology (see Introduction). These issues, however, are not the primary concern of this book. Indeed, scholars have also long noted the alliance between religion and capitalism from Weber's famous work The Protestant Ethic and the Spirit of Capitalism (1905) to Richard Roberts's Religion, Theology and the Human Sciences (2002). Such debates are important landmarks in our understanding of the relationship between capitalism and religion.

What we are suggesting here is not that religion can, or indeed should, be separated from economics and politics, but rather that neoliberal ideology is creating a globalising context in which a single model of the world – one dominated by economics and the values of the marketplace – is taking root. In this context 'religion' is being refashioned according to such a position.

> 'The most elementary forms of behaviour motivated by religious or magical factors are oriented to this world.'
>
> Max Weber, The Sociology of Religion, [1922] 1966, p. 1.

It is in the domination of an unrestricted market ideology that we find religion increasingly being interpreted in consumerist terms. In highlighting this we are not merely referring to the post-1960s supermarket 'pick and mix' approach to religions that we find within the various New Age movements and literature. As a social phenomenon this shift was consumer-oriented and generally presented itself in terms of de-traditionalisation, the exercise of personal free-dom and experimentation. What we are concerned with here is a relatively new development, linked to the deregulation of the markets in the 1980s, the collapse of the Soviet Empire in Eastern Europe and the process of globalisation, namely the corporate-led takeover of the cultural space of 'spirituality' and religion. Our primary concern then is with the reduction of what counts as 'spirituality' to a business ethos, as if something called 'spirituality' unquestionably supports privatisation or consumerist values or derives its significance from the benefits to be gained from maximising worker efficiency and/or production or profits. In drawing attention to this shift, we wish to challenge the way that corporate business is repackaging religion in terms of a 'spirituality' of consumerism (the earlier trend that it feeds upon) and corporate loyalty.

In the late 1990s there has been an explosion of literature on

business and spirituality and a celebration of 'spirituality' as
enhancing work performance. One conference on Women, Business
and Spirituality in 2002 declared spirituality 'the last taboo in
Corporate America' and expressed a desire to 'merge' spirituality and
business:

> Leaders in Corporate America must now address an area that affects
> human potential in the workplace – a need that is quietly, yet quickly,
> rising in importance among women employees and executives. It is one
> that is essential to the recruitment and retention of the best and
> brightest professional women. It is also controversial and evokes fear
> and scepticism among some decision-makers. It is, perhaps, the last
> taboo in Corporate America. *We call it spirituality.*
> (Women–Business–Spirituality: A New Formula for Leadership,
> New York City, 14 October 2002.)

It is precisely this 'merging' of 'spirituality' and 'business' that
obscures its objectives by masquerading as a consumer-led opportunity for individuals to express their freedom and individuality in the
religious/spiritual sphere of life. As such, it builds upon the modern
refashioning of the term 'spirituality' as an exclusively private reality,
but reorients the term in such a way that it now reflects *corporate*
not *individual* interests. While a large part of the literature on business
spirituality is about caring for employees and valuing human needs in
an ever more complex working environment, this is somewhat oddly
framed in terms of 'spirituality'. The values of human welfare and care
in business are without question extremely important, but what is
alarming is the uncritical utilisation of the idea of 'spirituality' – with
all of its semantic vagueness – as facilitating such a process. Those
wishing to utilise such a concept need to be aware of the way in which
the term 'spirituality' is increasingly being represented as *supporting* a
wider corporate ideology, rather than offering a corrective to it. Take,
for example, Georgeanne Lamont's *The Spirited Business* (2002). This
work, exemplifying a Quaker Reformist position, argues that 'soul-
driven' practices improve the working conditions of employees and
produce benefits for the corporate world. While the book embodies a
genuine attempt to improve the quality of working practice (an

extremely valuable activity) it uses the idea of 'spirituality' uncritically to frame such ideas. The book draws on a range of religious sources, with quotations from the Bhagavad Gita, Sufi traditions and the Dalai Lama, as well as various Christian texts. Interwoven between various descriptions of business working practice is a set of 'reflections' that attempt to put a 'spiritual' spin upon the business context. We are told in Lamont's discussion of the meaning of 'spirituality' that it is not about religion but about 'being fully alive, relationships and that which gives meaning and purpose to life' (p. 2). This 'Humpty-Dumpty' meaning allows for any set of vague generalities and non-specific allusions to religious wisdom to apply. However, at no point are these traditions shown to represent a challenge to the ethos and practices of corporate culture. The problem is that 'spirituality' is always portrayed as the friend of business and market values.

While observing business practices and the responses of individuals to the work environment, 'spirituality' is seen by Lamont to be present 'everywhere' and is principally concerned with valuing human beings and life in a working situation. In this context, with such a vague characterisation, 'spirituality' becomes little more than 'good working practice' with a glossy image. The vacuous nature of this use of 'spirituality' is shown by the way in which diverse historical and religious traditions are blended together according to a set of general working assumptions for good business practice. For example, Lamont's 'reflections' assume unanimity and collective agreement across a diverse range of traditions. 'Spiritual traditions', as a collective group of phenomena, are seen to speak with one voice and her 'reflections' are taken to be held in common by 'most spiritual traditions'. By erasing the diversity of religious traditions, a political position supporting capitalist ideology and practice can be generated. At times, Lamont does attempt to acknowledge that there are 'many forms of spirituality'. However, when rejecting ascetic models of spirituality as 'not the sort of spirituality that we are looking at in this book', it is never quite clear what kind of spirituality is being developed other than one that is non-specific and bland enough to support the underlying ethos of corporate culture. There are a few suggestions that Lamont's 'spirituality' questions the primacy of money (p. 116) and the global economic system (p. 281), but there is no real appreciation of the structural inequalities of corporate capitalism and the business culture that she describes. Despite noting the importance of charity, compassion and caring for others, Lamont somehow turns these values into internal factors for business success (a kind of 'enlightened self-interest'), and ignores the ways in which the corporate capitalist system maintains structural oppression, social injustice and world poverty. In consequence, Lamont's 'spirituality' at best abounds with contradictions, and at worst endorses the more pernicious aspects of capitalist spirituality. There is a clear sense, behind the valuable message about good working practices, that 'spirituality' is primarily about maximising profits and helping staff to achieve the company's financial goals. Thus, in *The Spirited Business*, Georgeanne Lamont suggests that

> When Microsoft's shares fell from $120 to $40 overnight it was the passion with which they believed in their vision – a vision of a world in which people connect – that helped staff to move through the discouragement and disappointment . . . Profit and soul go hand in hand as without the profits none of this compelling journey would be possible.
>
> (pp. 12, 72)

There is no doubt that Lamont seeks to bring important Quaker values to bear upon business practice, but the naive use of 'spirituality' as a marketing PR tool (she talks of the 'eight spiritual tools' as stillness, listening, story, encounter, celebration, grieving, visioning, journalling) is a denial of the social politics of 'spirituality' and does no more than create a brand name for her own management consultancy company 'SpiritWorks'.

The problem with Lamont's approach, and other reformist examples, is that they walk a fine line between ethical business and capitalist spirituality. Without an awareness of the wider political and cultural shift in the use of the term to support the corporate takeover of life, such works will inevitably blur the distinction between what are often two quite distinct ideological positions. The first (the ethical reformist) sees 'spirituality' and the 'religious' as an important corrective or countervailing force to the largely amoral world of economics. As for the latter, *capitalist spirituality uses spirituality and the religions to promote the corporate agenda of business*. As such, the reformists miss the silent takeover of religion and turn 'spirituality' into an added extra for improving consumption. Spirituality becomes in this instance a GMR – a Genetically Modified Religion – the tasty food additive that makes neoliberalism more palatable. In this 'brave new world' everything (including ideas or our own souls) can be genetically modified, patented and sold for profit. When the colonising powers tried to buy land from the native American populations of North America, the indigenous people were astonished to discover that you could buy and own land in the first place. How much more extraordinary to sell and market 'truth' and ways of life.

NEOLIBERALISM AND MANAGING YOUR EMPLOYEES – A SPIRITUAL GUIDE

In Chapter Two we considered the role that psychology has played in locating the religious within the private realm. In the previous chapter we have seen how this has created a powerful stereotype of Asian religions as mystical, otherworldly and individualistic. In the marketplace of the New Age 'religions of the self', ancient Asian wisdom traditions are translated into variants of something called 'eastern spirituality'. The meditative practices of these traditions, such as 'the inner technologies of the self' (*adhyatma vidya*) practised within Buddhism, are represented as leading to a *personal* enlightenment and the liberation of the individual practitioner from their own personal anxieties and sense of delusion. This privatisation allowed the emergence of individualised spiritualities that claim to represent the best of these Asian traditions for a western audience. Authors of books within the area of personal development, spirituality and 'mind, body and spirit' trade upon the exoticism, the ancient authenticity and the 'counter-cultural' image of such movements, while peddling philosophies that provide little more than an accommodation to mainstream western, consumerist culture. As we have seen, such popular literature actively misreads the transgressive and transformative potential of Asian wisdom traditions by interpreting their philosophical critique of the everyday individual self and the techniques for deconstructing our attachment to it, as 'cultivation of the self'. Ancient traditions, initially providing a community-oriented perspective and an 'other-directed' ethic, offer a profound challenge to our devotion to the personal self, but in a New Age context become commodified options within an overarching 'religion of the self'.

In more recent times we are seeing the development of a second mode of 'privatising' religion, this time influenced not by liberalism, which placed religion in the private space of individual choice, but by neoliberalism, which is *re-placing* religion (already disentangled from its institutional and cultural origins and repackaged as 'spirituality') into the corporate realm of business. We are essentially witnessing an attempted corporate takeover of the religions. This can be seen in the increasing tendency for the ancient and diverse religious traditions of the world to be simplified, homogenised, repackaged and then sold to consumers and business managers as ideologies promoting hedonism, business enterprise, work-efficiency, economic productivity and the values of a corporate business world. As Nigel Thrift (1997: 47) notes, such New Age 'spiritual training' is now big business in the corporate and management world:

> In the United States $4 billion per year is spent by corporations on New Age consultants, according to Naisbitt and Aburdene. For example, the New Age think tank, Global Business Network, is underwritten by major companies like AT&T, Volvo, Nissan, and Inland Steel. Some companies like Pacific Bell, Procter and Gamble, Du Pont and IBM, offer, or have offered, their employees 'personal growth experiences' in-house. Thus IBM provides 'Fit for the Future' seminars which introduce employees to the *I-Ching*. It is claimed that this links internal intuitions with external events. IBM's manager of employee development is quoted as saying that 'it helps employees understand themselves better' (Huczynski).

Thrift points out that New Age thinking appeals within management circles because it is eclectic and flexible, its emphasis upon personal development accords well with 'the rise of "soft" skills like leadership, intuition, vision and the like' and also because the New Age stress upon changing the individual fits well with management needs to adapt their workforce to changing market demands.

In contemporary society the discourse of 'spirituality' often promotes the ideology of neoliberalism in concealed and obscure fashions. Indeed, the very success of the term in the business and professional worlds is related to the way in which the notion of 'spirituality' acts as a kind of 'human-centred' safety-valve for corporate capitalism. It does this by providing an aura of authenticity, morality and humanity that mediates the increasingly pernicious social effects of neoliberal policies. Attention to an apparently 'spiritual dimension' of life allows workers to 'let off steam' when faced with increasingly oppressive and insecure job conditions.

This is achieved in a number of ways. First, by introducing 'spirituality' into the workplace, employees can be made to feel a sense of corporate community and allegiance to the company, obviating the increasingly dehumanising environment that they find themselves in as a result of the application of a purely economic or calculative rationality to their value to the company. This increasingly applies in all of the professions where the discourse of spirituality is taking hold. As Sophie Gilliat-Ray (2003: 344–5) notes with regard to the nursing context,

> The appropriation of spiritual care assessment and delivery, as advocated by many of the nursing writers, is precisely a mechanism for giving theoretical grounding to the claim that nursing is a profession, not simply an occupation. It is a form of social and professional capital . . . Many nurses receive low pay and experience low prestige. They work long and unsociable hours and there is a high turnover within the occupation . . . Not surprisingly therefore, the encouragement of nurses to engage in the spiritual care of patients can be a powerful antidote to occupational frustration.

Second, 'spirituality' provides the all-important 'feel-good' factor that is so important for improving worker efficiency and loyalty. Unlike the term 'religion', spirituality is a brand that is not tainted with a negative image. Third, those with a social conscience can buy into the idea of 'the spiritual' as somehow 'alternative', counter-cultural or subversive of mainstream materialistic values. Here 'spirituality' is sold to the consumer as a form of cultural critique, even if the form of spirituality that is usually offered is itself so commodified and entrenched within the system of consumption that it ends up support-ing the very system that at one level it appears to be challenging. Thus, while claiming to be 'alternative' (always an important value in establishing a niche in a competitive marketplace), the goal is to align the employee's 'personal mission' with that of the organisation for which they work. This of course is an attempt at thought-control, further facilitated through the use of 'mood-altering' techniques in staff development seminars devoted to exploring 'the spiritual dimension' of life (see Roberts, 2002: ch. 3). Colin Turner in his popular management book The Eureka Principle (1997: 45) argues that the search for meaning in life is 'the essential ingredient in organizational success'. Furthermore,

> The human resource paradigm of developing the individual does not go far enough. It needs to be transcended by an alternative that begins with *generating an understanding and belief of these unifying principles* . . . Through development of trustworthiness at an individual level and an *alignment of personal missions and values with those of the organization*, key individuals can then in turn influence the wider teams and departments by their example.
>
> (Turner, 1997: 121, our italics)

Whether you call such practices 'spiritual', 'religious' or just plain old-fashioned 'mind-control', what we are witnessing here is the extension of the economic rationality of the marketplace into the realm of fundamental human beliefs. Why is it, for instance, that, despite better living conditions, numerous household appliances and 'labour-saving devices', and increases in personal wealth and con-sumer choice (for those who can afford it), people spend more time at work today than they did a generation ago, with less and less time either to enjoy the fruits of their labour or to spend time with their family? What motivates such self-sacrifice on behalf of one's job? R. W. Fevre (2000) argues that this social phenomenon relates to the increasing application of a narrowly instrumental and calculative rationality from the realm of economics to all aspects of life. In effect the 'bottom line' has become the only line, and the Market has become the guiding force for all human relationships and actions as a whole.

> Capitalism – through the agency of the managerial class – has gradually persuaded employees to understand their work in the category of human belief and so to bestow on it a devotion which can have no rational payoff . . . [M]odern managers endeavour to make their employees think that work can be understood with human-belief logic. It is their aim to confuse us with a mixture of economic rationality – this is all being done in the name of our bottom line and your bank balance – and the spiritual. They introduce us to the ersatz morality that will measure our worth in terms of the hours we spend at work (and away from our loved ones).
>
> (Fevre, 2000: 213–4)

According to Escrivà da Balaguer, founder of the conservative Catholic movement, Opus Dei, 'To be holy means to sanctify work itself, to sanctify oneself in work, and to sanctify others with work' (Estruch, 1996: 245). The following account provides a good example of the way in which such notions of spirituality contribute to the greater productivity of employees:

> Manuel is a Catalan industrialist, father of an engineer who joined Opus Dei while still a student. After visiting one of the Work's centers and discovering its spirituality, Manuel said: 'Today I have discovered the best thing of my life, this suits me; *I have worked like a dog*, frantically, doing nothing else, and now I discover that by working I can also sanctify myself. This is fantastic!'
>
> (Estruch, 1996: 240, cited in Woodhead and Heelas, 2000: 185)

Like the discourse of 'excellence' and 'measurable accountability' that now pervades educational, public service and professional institutions throughout Europe and the USA, 'spirituality' acts as a 'positive,' but largely vacuous, signifier for 'personal development' and business enhancement. The rhetorical beauty of such discourses is that they effectively silence debate and criticism, by framing all dissent as unprogressive. Thus, rejection of the discourse of professional 'excellence' among employees is often presented by managers as 'resistance to accountability'. What such resistance often represents however is not a rejection of *accountability* as such but rather a rejection of a narrow logic of *accountancy* with regard to such processes. We find similar moves whenever individuals express resistance to 'spiritual values'. If 'spirituality' implies all that is 'sugar and spice and all things nice' that has been filtered out of the 'snips and snails and puppy-dogs' tails' of the traditional religions, then to be critical of the concept is like rejecting 'being a virtuous person' or equivalent to being against 'inner personal development'. Who would dare to say that they are against 'excellence' or 'spirituality' when defined in these terms? The danger however is that 'spirituality', when used in this vague and uncritical manner, ends up acting like a food colouring or additive that masks the less savoury ingredients in the product that is being sold to us. What is happening here with the concept of 'spirituality' of course is a classic case of the streamlining, downsizing and stripping of assets. This time however the assets are cultural (i.e. the religions are the target) rather than material in nature.

THE 'NEW' MARKET IDEOLOGY AND THE BRANDING OF SPIRITUALITY

Why is this takeover of religion by business enterprise occurring now?

In *The New Marketing Manifesto* (2000) John Grant, following the ideas of social theorists like David Riesman and Anthony Giddens, argues that there are three ages of branding. First, the 'trademark', at the turn of the twentieth

> 'Market logic promised universal salvation.'
>
> R. Laurence Moore, *Selling God: American Religion in the Marketplace of Culture*, Oxford University Press, 1994, p. 271.

century, where a product represented 'quality, reliability and safety'; second, the age of 'aspiration', roughly from the 1930s to the 1950s, where the brand reflected the buyer's social ideals and desire for certain values connected with the product, promoting a need to 'keep up with the Joneses'. Finally, Grant argues that we are now seeing the third age of branding, where the boundary between brands and other parts of culture disappears. This is the age of 'inward ideas' where 'brands are the new traditions'. According to Grant, following the breakdown of traditional society and 'tradition loss', individuals are 'tradition hungry', in the sense of 'needing ideas to live by'. In such a situation the corporate world is now in a position to step in and provide such meanings.

> Culture and media's main role has become meeting this hunger for meaning and order. Rather than simply elaborating as in past ages, culture is now needed to fill great gaps of meaning in our lives, which is ironic because it was modern media which undermined traditional ideas as much as any shift in patterns of living and working . . . This is why branding is such a powerful force in modern societies. Brands, achieving popular acceptance, shape people's lives in ways that brands never used to. Brands used to be ornamental . . . Now the brands, as ideas that we 'buy into', are a much freer force of transformation. They are instrumental.
>
> (Grant, 2000: 15)

The 'new' marketing philosophy is that brands now play the role of traditions by 'providing people with ideas to live by'. Brands effectively become 'popular ideas'. Grant does not see these as propaganda because their take-up is said to be voluntary and will only be successful if they meet the needs of a society. This is at best rather naive in that the 'needs of society' are themselves shaped by the cultural Zeitgeist. We now see how corporate capitalism begins to operate according to the traditional role of religious institutions in providing meaning and order. *Capitalism in effect is the new religion of the masses − the new opium of the people − and neoliberalism is the theological orthodoxy that is facilitating its spread.*

If Grant is correct in his analysis, then we can see how consumerism and the demands of corporate capitalism have become the new space of meaning, all the more sinister for the selective and dismissive way in which they use cultural and religious traditions as

> 'Religious suffering is the expression of real suffering and at the same time the protest against real suffering. Religion is the sigh of the oppressed creature, the heart of a heartless world, as it is the spirit of spiritless conditions. It is the opium of the people.'
>
> Karl Marx, *Toward the Critique of Hegel's Philosophy of Law,* 1843, p. 250.

resources to support the 'branding' of life for corporate gain. Religious traditions have become brands under the rubric of modern conceptions of 'spirituality' and the business world is increasingly exploiting the opportunity to market such ideas within the corporate structure of their organisations and within society as a whole. One of the ironies here is that it is the religious traditions themselves that are in the best position to provide alternative conceptions of 'spirituality' and resist the neoliberal takeover. However, by merging 'spirituality' with business and the market the power of such resistance is severely undermined. As the references in Grant's book to the British 'New' Labour Party demonstrate, 'politics' has also come under the regime of branding and marketing ideas through the manipulation of facts and truth – the culture of spin and perception.

It is striking that Grant sees no ethical problem resulting from his diagnosis of modern marketing and indeed celebrates the closer linkage of brands with 'everyday life'. Following survey work by North American psychologists and the work of Maslow (see Chapter Two), Grant encourages us in his second rule of new marketing to 'tap' (read: *exploit*) basic human needs. He lists fifteen basic human drives as: sex, hunger, physicality, avoiding distress, curiosity, honour, order, vengeance, social contact, family, prestige, power, citizenship, independence and social acceptance. What is perhaps interesting to ask is how many of these basic needs are undermined by a corporate world that is trying to 'tap' into such human needs in order to make money. And we should be under no illusions – the key feature of markets is to make money and not to respond to human welfare issues. The lack of ethical concern shown by Grant here is alarming. Consumerism knows no limits and human experience has now become a product like everything else.

Grant does not believe that the list of basic human needs provided by the psychologists he follows is in any sense perfect. There is, for instance, 'no mention of the human drive to religious ideas'. He appeals to psychology tests that show areas of the brain that 'glow when we think religious thoughts', itself another error of neuroscience in assuming that religion is a distinct, private and intense experience easily distinguishable from other dimensions of human life (see Chapter Two). Leaving this technical problem of the limits of neuroscience aside, Grant believes that an 'all pervasive spirituality' – including 'New Age sects, magical symbolism in computer games and alien abductions' – should be added to the list of basic drives that brands can 'attach to themselves' for market success (Grant, 2000: 38). The aim being to use (read: *exploit*) fundamental human needs and instincts for brand construction. By definition, as an important basic need or drive, 'spirituality' is open to the 'new' market philosophy. Grant does not explore the potential of 'spirituality' as a market product directly in his book, but he provides a wider framework for understanding how 'spirituality' is being used. Rule 4 of his 'new' marketing approach is 'Mythologise the New'. Loosely following Roland Barthes, he argues that 'mythology' can mean 'new traditions' and that branding is about creating such worlds. To mythologise is to integrate a social trend or aspects of life for market purposes.

> The new marketing approach is to offer brand ideas as a way of negotiating with new life situations. It means acting as the new traditions – not simply an addendum to the old ones. That is why I call it 'mythologizing'. It sounds a subtle distinction but I think it is quite a big shift to a more constructive role for marketing in society.
>
> (Grant, 2000: 12, 48)

Grant believes that there are constant opportunities for branding in contemporary society and that the 'loss of religion' is a fair target for the market. He argues that the 'spiritualised New Age from alternative therapy to Feng Shui and rave culture' is a 'profound trend' and one worth using. In his view, *The X-Files*, Playstation and Tango are brands that hold this quality, and he believes that there will be many more. Grant's third age of branding is symptomatic of the silent takeover of religion, and such 'new' marketing practices challenge religious traditions to examine carefully how their resources are being sold off in the service of such an ideology. It is the response to such new marketing ideologies and the plundering of the cultural resources of humanity for the sake of corporate profit that necessitates a critical perspective upon the modern phenomenon of 'spirituality'.

Mind, Body, Sales: God as CEO and 'Corporate Voodoo'

'Mind, Body and Spirit' products and books are big business. Business consultants Joyce Scanlon and Ann McLaughlin label this area the 'metaphysical market', offering solutions to life problems (see their website: www.ofspirit.com). They point out that the market vision behind this business is to provide relief from pain, whether emotional, physical or psychological. The potential buyers, classified across a spectrum from 'innovators' to 'sceptics', are identified according to their relative incorporation of the 'mind, body, spirit' (MBS) concept, and some are even rated according to their attitude towards 'spirituality'. It might be argued that business consultants help identify a legitimate market space and that an alliance between business and 'personal development' has an important role in distributing valuable services to needy people, but the real question is what kind of product is being sold. Offering therapy may have important individual and social values, but what if the goal is to sell business ideology itself as a form of 'spirituality'. This has been done in a number of ways and it is worth exploring how this operates in terms of confusing the link between business ethics and capitalist spirituality (which subordinates ethical reflections to an economic master).

Taking a religious tradition and using it for the benefits of business enterprise is perhaps, at the very least, an extremely limited use of a rich heritage. A tradition established for dealing with ethical issues of life and death is put to the narrow services of Capital. However, using religions is, according to Grant's model of 'new' marketing, a valuable way to sell a product. It also becomes a valuable way to make a product for business practice. Take an ancient religious idea and mythologise it (make a new tradition out of its raw material). In this way religious language, concepts and ideas can all be made in turn (with enough imagination and business flair) into a money-making exercise. This

> 'The "New Age" culture has become the largest pool of consumer suckers in history.'
>
> Bob Lozoff, *Just Another Spiritual Book*, Human Kindness Foundation, 1990, p. 76.

> '[M]any people crave a spiritual and goal-directed attitude in their companies.'
>
> Jesper Kunde, *Corporate Religion*, Prentice Hall, 2000, p. xii.

has happened in many ways from seeing God as the CEO to using the exoticism of Voodoo – a much-misunderstood tradition – to compete in the new market space. Business writers use the Christian message or Voodoo to build a corporate ideology (no ethical questions asked). The ironic aspect of this is that while both traditions would vehemently resist each other they are made to find common ground in their support for business ideology and the worship of capital. Thus, the British entrepreneur Richard Branson, the head of the Virgin corporation, advises that one should

> Build brands not around products but around reputation. The great Asian names imply quality and innovation rather than a specific item. I call these 'attribute' brands: they do not relate directly to one product – such as a Mars bar or a Coca-Cola – but instead to a set of values.
> (cited in Carayol and Firth, 2001: 22)

The so-called Protestant work ethic, with its Calvinist roots, has long inspired Christian groups to find ways of developing theological ideas to support business. Although much of this literature is not principally using the message of 'spirituality' we find the same drive to support business from the resources of the tradition. In this regard we find works recommending that the business ethos be shaped by the Christian message. Such an approach is often reformist in nature and does suggest some adaptation of the worst excesses of business practice according to Christian values, but the underlying message is that this will be beneficial to the business and provide the right ethical foundation. There is very little suggestion of a theological message that might challenge the self-interest of a capitalist approach or any reflections upon questions of social justice and a message that might question structural poverty. We thus find such works as Larry Julian's *God is My CEO: Following God's Principles in a Bottom-Line World* (2001) and Laurie Beth Jones's *Jesus, CEO: Using Ancient Wisdom for Visionary Leadership* (1995). In the latter work, Jesus is seen as the Chief Executive Officer (CEO) of a business providing and building on such qualities as strength in self-mastery, action and relationships. In the former case, while acknowledging a 'clash' between two worlds and tensions between 'people's needs and profit obligation', the aim of the book is always to find integration rather than question the terms set by the capitalist system and ideology. There is no ethical challenge in these works to the basic structures of capitalist neoliberalism. What we have instead is a 'reformist' moderation of business according to a highly selective reading of the Christian tradition.

Some, of course, are prepared to go much further in promoting a seamless link between capitalism and Christian belief. Consider for example the parish of Perimeter in Georgia, created in 1978 and owned by God Inc., an organisation with 32,000 members, 120 full-time employees and an annual budget in tens of millions of dollars. According to the Business and Finance manager of God Inc., Jerry Schriver, everything belongs to God and we are only the temporary managers of capital. Consequently, the mission of God Inc. is to integrate the Christian faith of its residents with their professional lives and the management of their personal finances. Each member of the community is therefore expected to give a minimum of 10 per cent of their income to the congregation. According to Schriver, this reflects biblical priorities: 'The Bible teaches us many things in this area. The theme of money recurs 2,312 times, while the theme of love is only mentioned 600 times' (cited in Bagot, 2003: 50).

In the Christian evangelical 'Bible Belt' in the USA it would be a marketing disaster to try to promote business practices by comparing corporate life to the ancient Haitian tradition of Voodoo, a tradition much maligned by Christian missionaries and Hollywood images of zombies. However, using 'exotic' traditions such as Voodoo alongside evangelical Christianity, reflects the 'new' market ideology where religion is nothing more than a tool for business and capital. In their book *Corporate Voodoo: Principles for Business Mavericks and Magicians* (2001) Rene Carayol and David Firth explain that Voodoo means 'mystery' and that corporate voodoo is 'the gateway to the magical'. It seeks to pick up the energy of the dynamic play of business, especially those who follow the 'natural', 'instinctive', 'risky', 'thrilling' and 'scary' business and are not afraid of failure. In the end, the message of 'Corporate Voodoo' seems to be that business is full of surprises and that we should be dynamic and resourceful in maintaining our competitive edge. Carayol and Firth here market a popular image of voodoo to promote corporate ideology and success through innovation and risk, with the aim of producing 'Fast business'. At one point they argue that 'Voodoo loves New Age financial engineering', giving Vodaphone and Orange and their competition with British Telecom as an example. Richard Branson is held up as a voodoo leader within business, as someone who takes risks with different products and companies, and the British supermarket chain Tesco is seen as holding the voodoo 'blend of experience and bravado' in their decision to set up internet shopping. It is never clear in the book how or why 'the liturgy' of voodoo relates to the people and traditions of Haiti, but the 'new mythology', to recall Grant, means that such concerns are of no importance. Voodoo, like Virgin, is a marketing tool, a brand name and a business group (The Voodoo Group). You can even buy 'The Voodoo Chill-Out Mix' on CD! Religion and values held within the traditions are redundant to the corporate religion of capital. corporate voodoo's displacement of tradition is seen by its use of insights from Osho and the Buddha, not to mention Winston Churchill. All religions are seen as meeting in the marketplace to worship the God of Capital. This is in effect a new *perennial philosophy* for a capitalist age. We may also note that in satirical fashion Naomi Klein's book *No Logo* is referred to by Carayol and Firth, but only to demonstrate a reader putting the book back and leaving the shop. Ethical and political reflection from the religious traditions, it appears, is not part of the 'new mythology'.

The Tao of Business: The Corporatisation of Taoism

No religious tradition is immune to the 'free market' ideology of neoliberalism. Whatever parts of the 'old traditions' can be siphoned off for use in the market will be used. As Daniel Bell (1979: 13–14) has noted,

> Modern culture is defined by this extraordinary freedom to ransack the world storehouse and to engorge any and every style it comes upon. Such freedom comes from the fact that the axial principle of modern culture is the expression and remaking of the 'self' in order to achieve self-realization and self-fulfillment. And in its search, there is a denial of any limits or boundaries to experience.

In this context every tradition from every part of the world is a potential resource for promoting corporate interests and the new God of
Capital. However, it is the Asian traditions, and 'Taoism' in particular,
which have seen the greatest market potential for 'New Age Capitalists'
in the West (Lau, 2000). This is because in a western context such
traditions can be more easily divorced from their cultural and institutional origins – in effect their 'brand-name' has not been tainted by
the unfortunate associations that still attach themselves to the traditional western religions. Moreover, since the dawn of Romanticism
and then again since the 1960s, 'eastern philosophies' have been
associated in the West with a kind of 'counter-cultural' exoticism that
makes them hip, fashionable and fresh for those looking around for
'alternative' philosophies in the competitive world of marketing.

As we saw in the previous chapter, the *Tao Te Ching* has often
been represented, particularly in the West, as a kind of anti-social
mysticism. There certainly is a tradition of Taoist hermits, cutting
themselves off from society, but again what we tend to see in the
modern era is the translation of Taoist philosophy into a privatised and
'secular' spirituality. The *Tao Te Ching* becomes a guidebook for getting
the job done, whether it is *The Tao of Management*, *The Tao of Sales* (how to
get on in business) or the *Tao of Sex* (how to have better sex with your
partner). Although the *Tao Te Ching* has become one of the primary
texts of New Age 'business spirituality' the text has a long history
of interpretation in China as a political treatise on how to rule a
kingdom. This should only surprise us if we assume that 'spiritual
wisdom' and politics are wholly separate realms, an assumption we
derive from the European Enlightenment. Indeed, the work was composed during the Warring States period of Chinese history (475–221
BC). This was a period where forty-four feudal states were reduced
to seven large and three small states and was marked by the rise of
statesmen and administrators, and a need for bureaucrats and political
advisors. This can be seen for instance in the text's critical attitude
towards belligerence and its clear preference for non-interference in
the affairs of other states. Military arms are of no use (ch. 30) and a
king should not seek to conquer others, for even the mighty will
inevitably topple!

The specific political dimension of the text and its social subversiveness (making it appealing to anarchist thinkers for instance) is erased in the management and sales approaches to Taoism and replaced instead by a capitalist emphasis upon individual and corporate success in the marketplace – doing well for yourself, getting promoted and being a more efficient worker for your employer. Consider for instance *The Tao of Sales: The Easy Way to Sell in Tough Times* by E. Thomas Behr (1997).

> This book brings the timeless principle of the *Tao Te Ching*, the Chinese philosophy of finding harmony in life, into the twenty-first century – and integrates them into the professional and personal lives of salespeople, business leaders, and entrepreneurs.
>
> (dustcover)

Fundamentally, Behr's text is about getting the edge on one's competitors in the cut and thrust of the global marketplace. The book advocates overcoming customer resistance to sales by transforming customers 'from opponents into allies'. In this way the ancient martial arts practice of using your opponent's own resistance as a means of overcoming them is advocated as a means of increasing sales. The book is organised into sections, each an attempt to read the significance of the ancient Taoist classic the *Tao Te Ching* for the contemporary entrepreneur. Similarly in his 1997 book, *The Eureka Principle*, Colin Turner uses the Taoist philosophy of the interplay of complementary opposites (*yin* and *yang*) to justify competitiveness and change as virtues in the marketplace. Turner (1997: 120) argues that 'Co-operation and competition are the Yin and Yang of the global marketplace and your organisation's culture is the one competitive advantage that cannot be duplicated.'

These kinds of readings are more Dow Jones than 'Dow-ism', and are a far cry from the original context of early Taoist thought, which advocates restraint, non-violence and the overcoming of the shackles of self-aspiration and individualism. According to the *Tao Te Ching*, the Taoist sage promotes the attainment of serenity through the eradication of desire for things and by a life of profound simplicity (37). This is said to be the wisdom of knowing what is enough and abusing nothing, of knowing when to stop and harming nothing (44). The Taoist sage rejects acquisitiveness, preferring instead the reward of helping others (81). Wealthy nobles are criticised in the text for owning expensive clothes and swords and growing fat through excessive consumption: 'Personal wealth is excessive. This is called thieves' endowment. But it is not Tao' (53). In contrast, the Taoist sage works to overcome competitiveness and desire:

> The Sage rules
> By emptying hearts and filling bellies,
> By weakening ambitions and strengthening bones,
> Leads people away from knowing and wanting
> Deters those who know too much from going too far
> Practices non-action
> And the natural order is not disrupted
> (from *Tao Te Ching* 3, all translations from Addiss and
> Lombardo, 1993)

The ideal in the Tao Te Ching then is precisely a rejection of an ethic of competitiveness (66). The values it upholds are compassion, frugality and humility (67). The text also contrasts the way of the Tao with the conventional attitudes of human society, advocating the giving of all surpluses to the poor, rather than lining the pockets of the rich:

> The Human Route
> Is not like this
> Depriving the poor,
> Offering to the rich.
>
> Who has a surplus
> And still offers it to the world?
> Only those with Tao
>
> Therefore the Sage
> Acts and expects nothing
> Accomplishes and does not linger
> Has no desire to seem worthy.
> (from *Tao Te Ching* 77, translation by
> Addiss and Lombardo, 1993)

Indian Wisdom meets Global Capitalism: The Affluence Gurus

Asian traditions such as 'Buddhism', 'Hinduism' and 'Taoism' represent a wide range of philosophies, practices, institutions and movements with a long and varied history. Despite our tendency to classify them as 'isms' – implying some degree of uniformity – they represent diverse and historically variable cultural phenomena – more like civilisations than 'religions' in our modern sense of the term. As such, we can find plenty of evidence of the involvement of practitioners and institutional representatives of these traditions in economic modes of exchange. Epigraphical evidence clearly demonstrates that historically the main financial donors at Buddhist pilgrimage sites in South Asia have been Buddhist monks, this despite the official monastic rule preventing individual monks from possessing wealth. Before the suppression of their economic networks by the British Raj at the end of the eighteenth century, Hindu ascetics and renouncers were often deeply involved in the social, economic and political activities of Indian communities, often acting as travelling soldier-mercenaries, traders and money-lenders. In a contemporary context we can point to a number of movements that teach that there is no conflict between material gain and spiritual advancement, from Buddhist groups like Nichiren Shoshu/Soka Gakkai (Japan and internationally), Fu Kwang Shan (Taiwan) and Dhammakaya (Thailand) to New Age teachers like Osho Rajneesh, Deepak Chopra and Maharishi Mahesh Yogi (Transcendental Meditation).

Lisa McKean's book *Divine Enterprise* (1996) provides many examples of the flourishing market in 'Hindu spirituality' in contemporary India. McKean offers an incisive critique of the profit-motives of many Hindu gurus and their complicity with a Hindu nationalist agenda. Her traditional Marxian approach, however, assumes from the start that there is a 'logic of asymmetrical exchange' in operation when a Hindu teacher is given money by his or her disciples. The materialist assumption in her work that there is no *real* exchange taking place assumes that western secular views of the world (such as Marxism and *crucially* most forms of capitalism) have some kind of unmediated access to 'what is really going on' and that only *material* exchanges are valuable. This view of the world is of course rather Eurocentric in presuming the 'disenchantment of the world' as reality. There is also an underlying assumption in the book that economics and spirituality should not really be mixed together. As our historical examples have shown, such a separation of the two spheres cannot be strictly maintained, especially in the South Asian context that McKean discusses. Nevertheless, McKean's work is important in calling into question the duplicity involved when Hindu gurus claim to have 'transcended material gain' at the same time as profiting from such claims. In a strikingly similar fashion to the trends we have been discussing, McKean argues that 'spirituality' acts as a means of 'socialisation from above'. This is not experienced as domination by members of society, she argues, because of 'spirituality's ideological effect', that is the way in which it transforms a sense of discomfort and a longing for meaning and value into a purely individualised realm of 'self-enlightenment'. This move deflects attention from issues of social injustice and poverty by privatising concern in terms of self-interest. Her work demonstrates rather well that the trends that we are discussing in this book are by no means exclusively western. Capitalist spirituality has truly gone global! As McKean (1996: 29) notes:

> Institutionalised spirituality neither denies nor dwells on the existence or experience of oppression based on economic exploitation. It reframes oppression as a problem amenable to solutions that promise individuals the means to experience transcendental truth.

What McKean's analysis ignores, however, is that at the same time as sanctioning the pursuit of wealth, all of the world's great religious traditions have also provided a powerful set of ideals, practices and disciplines for transcending individual self-interest and restraining the uncontrolled pursuit of one's desires. There are many contemporary movements within India that have a 'spiritual' emphasis to their socially engaged activity, such as the Sarvodaya (Welfare for All) communities inspired by Gandhian and Buddhist ideals, the Ambedkharite Buddhists of South India, Dalit liberation theology movements, etc. These groups seek to challenge structural and social inequalities and alleviate poverty and draw upon the same traditions (Hindu, Buddhist and Christian) that are being transformed into capitalist spiritualities elsewhere. As Stephen Batchelor has suggested in his discussion of Socially Engaged Buddhism this reflects an attempt to consider the consequences at the macro-level of the pursuit of self-interest. For such groups, he notes,

> practice is rooted in an awareness of how self-centred confusion and craving can no longer be adequately understood only as psychological drives that manifest themselves in subjective states of anguish. We find these drives embodied in the very economic, military and political structures that influence the lives of the majority of people on earth.
>
> (Batchelor, 1997: 112)

In North America probably the best known and most influential protagonist of what we are calling 'capitalist spirituality' is Deepak Chopra, best-selling author and exponent of Ayurveda, 'Quantum Healing' and the ultimate 'feel-good' spirituality for the affluent. Chopra has written over 30 books that have collectively sold in excess of 10 million copies and been translated into 25 different languages. His books include such works as *Ageless Body, Timeless Mind* (1993); *The Seven Spiritual Laws of Success* (1995); and *The Way of the Wizard or Creating Affluence* (1993). In 1999, *Time* magazine placed him in the top 100 icons and heroes of the twentieth century.

Like the UK's Barefoot Doctor, discussed in Chapter Three, Chopra's approach to 'eastern spirituality' has a strong emphasis upon a holistic mind-and-body approach to healing. Born in New Delhi in 1947, Chopra's initial training was in western medicine. Graduating from the All India Institute of Medical Sciences in 1968, Chopra moved to the USA in 1970, where he specialised in internal medicine and endocrinology, becoming chief of staff at the New England Memorial Hospital. He became increasingly disillusioned with the limitations of western (allopathic) medicine and embarked upon an exploration of South Asian Ayurvedic traditions as a means of developing a more integrated and holistic approach. In 1991 Chopra founded the American Association of Ayurvedic Medicine, before relocating to California and establishing the Chopra Centre for Well Being in La Jolla, California, in 1995, where he serves as educational director. According to Vijay Prashad (2000: 48),

Chopra . . . is the Vivekananda of the New Age. [He] fails even to
mention the structural poverty of his homeland, nor does he offer any
type of criticism of capitalism as Vivekananda did. He is now the
complete stereotype willed upon India by U.S. orientalism, for he
delivers just what is expected of a seer from the East. Chopra offers
a way to be a better consumer and person within the system . . .

Chopra's published works and lectures are an eclectic mix of traditional Indian Ayurveda ('the science of life'), Indian philosophical
ideas, meditation techniques and classic New Age interests such as the
apparently 'spiritual' and 'holistic' implications of quantum physics.
The underlying philosophy of Chopra's work seems to be a kind of
Neo-Vedantic search for self-knowledge, grounded in a belief in the
unity and universality of consciousness manifested in diverse forms
and levels. This philosophy, however, takes something of a back seat to
Chopra's main concerns, which have been to promote an integrated
'mind–body' approach to health treatment aimed at reversing (or at
least deferring) the ageing process and 'freeing' individuals to pursue
their own happiness and fulfil their innermost desires.

Chopra is as controversial as he is successful. He has been criticised
by physicists for his attempt to interpret quantum mechanics in
terms of consciousness (itself a popularised version of Niels Bohr's
famous 'Copenhagen interpretation') and by Christian evangelicals for
what they see as the covert promotion of Hindu religious ideas within
his books. This of course has not prevented Chopra from being
immensely successful, charging thousands of dollars for giving talks
and consultations to politicians and business leaders. Success in life,
according to Chopra, can be defined as the continued expansion of
happiness and the progressive realisation of one's goals. He argues, for
instance, in *The Seven Spiritual Laws of Success* that actions motivated by love
cause a multiplication of energy. This surplus energy can then be
channelled 'to create anything that you want, including unlimited
wealth'. According to Susan Bridle, who interviewed Chopra for the
popular New Age magazine *What is Enlightenment*, Chopra's success 'lies
in his simultaneous appeal to the forces of materialism and narcissism
that drive so many of us'. She continues:

> Chopra promises that we can fulfil all our worldly desires, desires that the great wisdom traditions have repeatedly reminded us are the very source of endless suffering and ignorance – desires for immortality, unlimited wealth and unending romance, all without having to struggle or make effort in any way. . . . Rather than recognizing spiritual transformation as an ultimately demanding endeavor, as taught by the greatest sages, Chopra popularises the notion of an easy, feel-good spirituality, with no mention of the perennial spiritual imperatives of renunciation and one-pointed dedication. And rather than emphasizing that true spiritual life is and has always been about the death of the ego, Chopra teaches us to bend the power of the infinite to our own will. . . . Chopra's brand of spirituality is like fast food; while it seems to satisfy, it actually numbs the very hunger that inspires the spiritual quest in the first place.
>
> (Bridle, 2001)

Chopra's reply to the charge that he is promoting consumerism and individualistic acquisitiveness in the course of Bridle's interview is reminiscent of other New Age gurus of the late twentieth century such as Osho Rajneesh. The problem, we are told, is not wealth as such but our attachment to it:

> materialistic values are not bad. The idea that spirituality must be divorced from material success is one of the things that has kept India in poverty and dependent on the rest of the world throughout these centuries. It comes from that interpretation of spirituality. . . . the spiritual path, if you consider it demanding, you will make it demanding. You will be very serious about it and you'll never get anywhere. I really think that what is required is easiness, comfort and not taking yourself too seriously.
>
> (Deepak Chopra, cited in Bridle, 2001)

This of course begs the question as to why such figures devote so much time and energy to justifying the acquisition of that which they reputedly have no real interest in. Chopra's response also displays a myopic view of recent Indian history that completely ignores the economic exploitation of the subcontinent in an age of European colonialism. Such historical and political myopia is a key feature of what we are calling *capitalist spirituality*.

The Indian guru Osho Rajneesh (1931–90) offered a radical and highly eclectic brand of spirituality that mixed western psychology with the teachings of various Asian wisdom traditions. Always quixotic and iconoclastic, Osho represented a contemporary blend of Neo-Tantra (promoting sexual experimentation as a means of overcoming desire and achieving enlightenment), Hindu non-dualism ('we are all God') while also borrowing liberally from the Mahayana Buddhist (especially Zen) and Taoist traditions. Rajneesh first came to public attention in Poona, India, in the 1970s where he was labelled 'the Sex Guru', because of his unorthodox teaching methods, his contrarian polemics against traditional religions in India and especially for his promotion of the exploration of one's spirituality through sexual experimentation. Perhaps not surprisingly, Rajneesh attracted many followers intrigued by his teaching and charismatic style. Soon large numbers of affluent, white westerners flocked to his Ashram in Poona. According to Rajneesh,

> They don't belong to me, those cars – nothing belongs to me. I am the poorest man in the whole world, living the richest life possible. My people love me; they want to do something for me. All those cars belong to the commune. They have made them available to me for one hour each day. I don't know which car they are bringing, but one thing is certain, that I can be comfortable only in a Silver Spur. And they love me so much that they are trying to have three hundred and sixty-five Rolls Royces, one for every day. And I say, 'Why not? A great idea!'
>
> (Osho Rajneesh, see
> http://www.oshoturk.com/osho-life/08-20-rolls.htm)

As Judith Fox, notes, although Rajneesh seems to have lived in a one-room apartment during his first period in Poona, he had already established a reputation for flamboyance, with a penchant for jewel-encrusted Rolex watches and the St Laurent towel that his devotees had given to him. She notes that:

Bhagwan characteristically explained that the automobiles, watches, and other evidence of opulence were devices to attract the curious by challenging their fixed ideas. Those who agreed with him included the American novelist Tom Robbins, who later observed that Bhagwan's path '. . . twists through the topsy-turvy landscape of the Ego as Joke. Of course, a lot of people don't get the punchline. (How many, for example, realise that Bhagwan's ridiculous fleet of Rolls Royces was one of the greatest spoofs of consumerism ever staged?)' [cited in George Meredith, *Bhagwan: The Most Godless Yet The Most Godly Man*, Rebel Publishing House, 1989, p. x]. Such excesses were perceived by critics as inflammatory, especially given the poverty that existed in the streets around the ashram.

(Fox, 2002: 19–20)

In the 1980s, Rajneesh moved his roadshow to the USA, setting up a self-sufficient community known as Rajneeshpuram in the state of Oregon. In North America Rajneesh became known as 'the Rolls Royce Guru' because of his penchant for such vehicles (at one time he owned over ninety of them and hoped eventually to own one for each day of the year). Every day 'the Bhagwan', or Osho as he later preferred to be called, would be driven through his city in one of his expensive cars, allowing his adoring disciples to gain a brief 'darshan' of their teacher. Eventually, Rajneeshpuram collapsed under the weight of criminal activities by a minority of its members, internal power-struggles among Osho's key followers, and intense pressure from local and federal government agencies to close the commune down. Despite his death in 1990, the Osho group continues to make between $15 million to $45 million per year in the USA from corporate clients such as BMW, providing opportunities for stressed executives to 'release anger from their systems' (Prashad, 2000: 62–3).

Compared to Chopra, Rajneesh was anti-establishment and anarchic in his approach to spiritual teaching. He was a prolific author and his previous training as a philosophy lecturer can be seen in the in-depth way in which he engages with many of the philosophical ideas contained within the various Asian wisdom traditions from which he drew inspiration. Rajneesh's strategy of challenging traditional dichotomies by bringing 'spirituality' into the world is reminiscent of the Buddhist example of the wealthy layman Vimalakirti (see Chapter Three). The influence of Mahayana Buddhist ideas is striking throughout Osho's many writings, not only in his rejection of a separation of liberation (nirvana) from living in the world (samsara) but also in the emphasis Osho placed upon 'Zen themes' (or rather the iconoclastic and mystical image of Zen that has been popularised in the West in the twentieth century). He freely used western psychological therapies and techniques in his workshops and encouraged experimentation by his disciples. His 'shock tactic' meditation techniques were designed to unlock a kind of inner spontaneity and Dionysian spirit within each practitioner that reminds one of Taoism and Friedrich Nietzsche. It is clear, however, from his choice of the term 'Sannya' to refer to his followers (from the traditional Hindu term sannyasin – renouncer), the use of Sanskrit names to refer to each newly ordained disciple, and his fundamental belief that 'everything is divine consciousness' that Rajneesh's primary influences remained much closer to his own Indian origins – namely the non-dualistic philosophies of Hindu Vedanta and Neo-Tantra.

> I want to unite the sannyasin with the world. I want sannyasins who
> work on farms and in factories, in offices and shops right in the
> marketplace. I don't want sannyasins who escape from the world;
> I don't want them to be renegades from life. I want them to live as
> sannyasins in the very thick of the world, to live with the crowd amid
> its din and bustle. Sannyas will have verve and vitality if the sannyasin
> remains a sannyasin in the very thick of the world.
>
> (Osho Rajneesh, September 1970,
> http://www.oshoturk.com/osho-life/06-02-sannyas.htm)

In the broadest possible terms both Rajneesh and Chopra remain within the spectrum of Hindu Vedantic/Tantric thought with their emphasis upon a divine consciousness pervading all of reality. However, they are very different personalities and for that reason probably appeal to slightly different audiences. Both figures embrace the business world, but whereas Chopra would not look out of place in a boardroom or in a pinstriped suit, Osho was very much in the tradition of the charismatic Indian guru, with long white beard, piercing stare and flowing Indian robes. Chopra offers an easy, accessible and not too discomforting spirituality that promotes individual and corporate success with little cost to a modern western consumerist lifestyle. Rajneesh sought to shock and challenge and expected a much greater engagement with Asian wisdom traditions among his followers. However, what is lacking in Rajneesh's otherwise challenging corpus of works and lectures is any real reference to the social and political structures which prevent people from attaining the enlightenment that he taught. There is no critique of 1980s corporate culture in his work or of the effects of consumerism and a lack of social justice in the world. When other-directed virtues such as compassion and concern for others are mentioned these are generally presented as potentially positive side-effects of the experience of enlightenment, rather than as the goal one is seeking to achieve (as in, say, the Mahayana ideal of the *bodhisattva*).

In that sense Osho, provided the perfect 1980s repackaging of 'Asian spirituality' themes from the counter-cultural alternative scene of the 1960s. This time, however, there is no requirement to drop out or overcome your desires. Consumption and the pursuit of wealth became techniques for attaining enlightenment itself. This message was exactly what a generation of ex-hippies who now worked in the boardrooms of corporate America in the acquisitive Eighties wanted to hear. Although there is clearly a precedent for such practices within certain strands of Hindu Tantra (where the attainment of enlightenment is to be achieved by working through your desires rather than by suppressing them), the potentially radical elements in Rajneesh's philosophy are undermined by his privatised blend of western psychological discourse and Asian wisdom. The result, as we have seen from examples in earlier chapters, is a domestication of Asian philosophies according to the ideologies of contemporary consumerism and individualising psychologies. Enlightenment becomes an individual matter of self-transformation rather than a matter of *overcoming* of self. This is not to say that Rajneesh's approach does not have potentially subversive elements within it, but rather that in focusing so exclusively upon the individual, the Rajneesh movement as a whole has tended to accommodate itself to the mainstream rather more than its members may have realised. This is perhaps another example of how the subtle acceptance of a psychological discourse for interpreting Asian philosophies domesticates a potentially anarchic and iconoclastic worldview in such a way as to promote an individualised religion of the self. As Margaret Thatcher observed so poignantly during the same period of the acquisitive 1980s, the way to transform people's souls is through economics – to transform them into individuals – that is to erase the social dimensions of their 'spirituality'. The problem with the contemporary conjunction of business and spirituality in such cases as Osho and Chopra is that business remains the master and 'spirituality' merely the tool for achieving greater efficiency, individual success and corporate profitability.

Clearly, Rajneesh did not see a problem with the conjoining of individual wealth-acquisition and spiritual advancement. As we have seen, all of these themes can be found in the various Asian wisdom traditions from which Rajneesh draws some of his inspiration. Much of his teaching is oriented towards challenging conventional religious assumptions about 'other-worldliness' and the power of mainstream religious ideologies to control people's desires and natural spontaneity. In Rajneesh, however, there is a strong Nietzschean influence that is critical of the 'mind-control' and constricting moralities of mainstream religion. However, Rajneesh appears to have missed the fact that the new religion in town that required confrontation by his iconoclastic approach was not traditional Christian sexual morality, or Hindu asceticism or institutionalised Buddhism, but rather the religion of the Market.

> To me, a capitalist society is a natural phenomenon. A socialist structure is not natural. It is something imposed, something conceived of through the mind. Capitalism developed by itself; socialism has to be brought about, it cannot come by itself.
>
> (Osho Rajneesh, *The Eternal Quest*, 15, see http://www.oshoturk.com/osho-life/06–31-predictions.htm)

[I]f capitalism is developed properly, socialism will be its natural
outcome – in a pregnancy of nine months the child comes out of its
mother's womb naturally and silently. So, talk of socialism when
capitalism has not yet grown to its full height, is suicidal. . . . Socialism
will stem from capitalism if the latter is allowed its full growth. But
capitalism should go only after it has completed its job.

(Osho Rajneesh, April 1970,
http://www.oshoturk.com/osho-life/05–42-socialism.htm)

Flourishing in the consumerist spirit of 1980s Anglo-American politics
and culture, Rajneesh benefited from the prevailing individualism of
the time and he seemed unable to step back and be sufficiently critical
of this trend. Influenced by Maslow's notion of a hierarchy of human
needs (i.e. that it is only once one has attained basic material comforts
that the search for spirituality really begins, see Chapter Two),
Rajneesh deliberately targeted the affluent with his teachings. The
message, however, involved little consideration for the poor of society
and tended to promote individual freedom and worldly accommodation to consumer capitalism rather than offering a challenging
critique of it. The future of the Osho movement, claiming as it does a
radical and revolutionary approach to spiritual enlightenment, will
depend to a large extent upon the ability of its members to read its
own sacred teachings (the writings and lectures of Osho) in terms of
a wider social ethic which challenges mainstream values. Without
this, the Osho movement will be little more than a denomination of
capitalist spirituality – the new religion of the self, in its largely
uncritical promotion of a feel-good spirituality of consumerism,
individual self-fulfilment and corporate success.

CORPORATE RELIGION: MAKING MONEY FROM CONCEPTS

Brands will become religions and some individuals, who are seen as an
expression of their brands, will themselves become religions.

Jesper Kunde, *Corporate Religion*, 2000, p. 6

The use of specific religious traditions is not the only way that the
market seeks to take over religion. The very concept of 'religion' –
itself a problematic taxonomic category (see King, 1999a and

Fitzgerald, 2000) – is mythologised for business culture. Bringing together ideas of corporate and brand religion Jesper Kunde in his work *Corporate Religion* (2000) seeks to show that companies need an ethos or belief-system to be effective and efficient. Much of the language of corporate religion echoes a Christian missionary emphasis upon evangelism and a strong belief in the company, religious leaders, visions and missions. Religion for Kunde (2000: 2) is 'binding together in a belief'. He argues that, in a changing and unpredictable world, companies require the strength of a corporate religion and a 'vision' to carry the company forward in a competitive context. As John Grant indicated, it is concepts (ideas) that create international markets and by developing a 'religious ethos' a company can build not only a strong identity but also a powerful structure of 'spiritual management'. Kunde (2000: 8) argues that

> What takes a company to success is its philosophy, articulated by a
> 'spiritual' management. . . . Spiritual management is set to become
> the most important management tool of the future, because it provides
> the only protection against the complexity of new products and the
> speed of market change.

The key idea here is that it is 'emotional' values that will determine the success of a product and company. Such 'corporate religions' include Microsoft, the Coca-Cola Company, Nike, Harley-Davidson, Virgin, Walt Disney and the Body Shop. Kunde accepts that consumers are not robots and therefore require 'added value' not just in terms of an emotional connection to the product but also a 'belief' – one in fact that will shape the ethos of the entire company. This belief unifies the company, offering employee-focus and the opportunity for inspired leaders to provide 'strong management' within the company and to cultivate what he calls 'spiritual management'. In line with Weber's emphasis upon charismatic leadership in the formation of religious movements, Kunde sees businessmen like Richard Branson and Bill Gates as displaying the qualities of religious leaders. Bill Gates, he argues, 'is an outstanding example of a spiritual leader who uses the media to control both his company and the business area in which Microsoft operates' (Kunde, 2000: 8).

Kunde outlines five trends within 'spiritual management', moving from a national to an international basis and from a basic product to a belief system. By associating the product with something larger than itself a distinction can be made between the generic product and what is actually being sold (2000: 64). This belief aspect provides a firm foundation that enables the company to become an international force by selling a value with the product. It is the increasingly international dimension involved in transmitting the values of a brand and the new 'corporate religions' that demonstrates why the deregulation of the global market (or more accurately the regulation of world markets for the benefit of a few leading companies) is the beginning of a corporate takeover of religious traditions. Through such processes religious systems and traditions are 'merged' in a manner that makes them fundamentally supportive of the single truth of neoliberalism. The religious ethos that Kunde identifies is at one level an illuminating analogy, but at another level it reflects a clear ideological shift at the end of the twentieth century and the increasing adoption of 'religion' as a marketing tool for spreading capitalist ideology. One could say that works such as those of Kunde and Grant are classic examples of capitalist wish-fulfilment and that they exaggerate the impact of corporations and the market upon our lives. However, as David Loy (2002: 208) notes,

> According to the U.N. Development Report for 1999, the world spent at least $435 billion the previous year for advertising, and according to the Worldwatch Institute almost half was spent in the United States alone. . . . *this constitutes the greatest effort in mental manipulation that humanity has ever experienced* – all of it to no other end than creating consumerist needs for the sake of corporate profit. No wonder a child in the developed countries consumes and pollutes thirty to fifty times as much as a child in the Third World, according to the UNDR 1999. While 270 million 'global teens' inhabit a single pop-culture world, consuming the same designer clothes, music and soft drinks, almost a billion people in seventy countries consume less today than twenty-five years ago.
>
> (our italics)

The adoption of religious language by the business world is part of a set of power shifts away from what Kunde calls *faith* traditions towards what we can call the *faith in capital* tradition (the corporate religion). Kunde draws a direct comparison with the Roman Catholic Church and argues that such a 'worldwide organisation of faith which has created an enormous commitment from its global congregation' shows that 'faith breeds motivation' (2000: 164). This is an extraordinary admission to make – namely that powerful multinational companies are now trying to use what they see as the key persuasive tools and strategies of the religions as a means of improving their power and market position. Kunde also claims that it is possible to create a corporate religion within a single year, according to his ten-point timetable of implementation. During the period of implementation 'the religious leader must be highly visible' and 'the religion must be impressed on everybody right from the start'. This sense of control is emphasised at the end of Kunde's work when he acknowledges that 'religions can be powerful forces' and for this reason 'must be carefully controlled' (2000: 249). Here we see the hidden power of 'spiritual management'. Traditional religions are rejected in the spirituality literature as being too institutional and authoritarian, but companies are now using similar structures to promote the product of spirituality! Kunde's work shows how concepts and values shape human behaviour and the way in which the 'new' corporate religion challenges older traditional values. This is more than an analogy; it is the marketing of religion for the sake of capitalism. In many ways Kunde's work has an honesty which much of the New Age market denies in the decorations of its philosophy, but both reflect the pervasive takeover of religion.

AUDITING RELIGION AND THE CORPORATE UNIVERSITY

Most academics seem to have passed uncomprehending and silent to their intellectual slaughter; fatally they have neglected to investigate, in accordance with the canonical criteria of their own vocation, that is with critical and above all, *critically reflexive* thought, the weapons of the enemy.

(Roberts, 2002: 105)

If, as we are arguing, the religions are being plundered, repackaged and then sold to us as 'spiritualities' that teach us to conform, why are we not hearing more about this in the form of protests and alternative perspectives? There are a number of responses to this question. First, we are seeing increasing resistance to these trends, most publicly through the activities of anti-capitalist protests and groups (in and outside 'religious' institutions) with a social conscience. This has usually been presented to us in the media as an economic and political struggle rather than a *religious* one, though this is the usual story of compartmentalising dynamic social trends. At an ideological level, the struggle between corporate capitalism on the one hand and citizen and community rights on the other, is a struggle over rival cosmologies, worldviews and visions of humanity's future. Second, most of the commentators and spokespersons for the anti-capitalist movement in the West have tended to articulate the movement's resistance in narrowly socio-political terms. Moreover, many of the left-wing groups and figures mobilised in these situations remain highly suspicious of any references to 'religion' or 'spirituality'. More generally, we should be aware that the saturation of contemporary culture in the language of the market is such that it has the tendency to silence the articulation of difference, as our ability to 'think otherwise' becomes disabled by the colonisation of our thought-processes.

The takeover of religion by capitalist spirituality is also being silently promoted in educational institutions and by academic experts in the study of religion who have the potential to provide a critical response to the commodification of religious traditions. More than ever before, it is now possible to see market forces shaping the form and content of the study of religion in universities, colleges and schools. Market demand for courses shifts academic concerns and the asking of difficult questions about the world. University courses are set according to market demand and academics produce courses tailor-made to meet such fiscal concerns. As Richard Roberts so poignantly indicates, education has become 'the processing of student bio-mass', it is concerned with units of assessment and budgets rather than the nature and quality of thinking itself.

In such a climate, 'spirituality' flourishes as a new 'brand' to be dutifully consumed by Thatcher's and Reagan's children, who can no longer revolt because they are trapped by credit and loans that pacify them into educational submission. For many students in this context, their primary concern is to do no more than the conveyor belt of knowledge requires of them and replicate the images presented to them in the mimetics of 'religious' knowledge. Students want to hear about 'spirituality', they want to hear the truth of its privatisation and to use 'religious' categories in the way they have received them in mainstream popular culture. Less and less are we encouraged to think that things might be interpreted other than they appear, or disturbed into thinking that ideas like 'spirituality' might function as a political tool in the hands of government, business managers or conservative academics. The orientation of students co-opted by this neoliberal system is to consume an idea without thinking critically about it. To consume without rebellion. As George Ritzer, sociologist and author of *The McDonaldisation of Society*, notes in an interview in *The Times Higher Education Supplement,*

> McDonaldised universities are set up precisely *not* to give their
> students the freedom to think for themselves. . . . Dehumanisation and
> depersonalisation are becoming the main feature of McDonaldised
> education. Students don't want to talk to me about ideas, only about
> grades. They're used to the drive-in and the ATM, and this spills over
> into their lives. They want to drive past their tutors. They want you to
> feed them bite-sized McNuggets of information.
>
> (George Ritzer, 20–27 December 2002)

In a context of limited financial resources (caused in the UK context at least by the rolling back of state provision in the funding of higher education), courses on 'religion' become 'shopping' outlets for popular brands. With the modern university more and more modelled on the business corporation, selling one's subject takes place in an internal market of competition with other academic subject areas. To attract the 'consumer' to your particular brand (degree subject and course), academics are increasingly being required to provide accessible, packaged and 'sexy' modules. Potentially challenging but enriching topics, themes and approaches become marginalised in the pursuit of student numbers. 'Would you like French Fries with your degree, or perhaps you would like to "go-large" with a Masters?' The problem in such a consumerist context is how to encourage critical thinking in a system that encourages conformity and is increasingly driven by 'the bottom line' of financial accumulation and market dominance. In a highly bureaucratised culture of outcomes, targets and goals, teachers and students work according to a conveyor belt mentality of production and approach the study of religion as if simply acquiring 'the basic facts' (knowledge as information) is what is required, rather than pausing to ask fundamental questions about life and challenging the fabric of thought itself (knowledge as wisdom). As David Loy (2002: 200) notes,

> As a professor of philosophy and religion I know that whatever I can do with my students a few hours a week is practically useless against the proselytizing influences that assail them outside class: the attractive (often hypnotic) advertising messages on television and radio and in magazines and buses etc., that constantly urge them to 'buy *me* if you want to be happy.'

As corporate business and high-street consumers promote 'spirituality', so students require courses on 'spirituality' that reinforce, sometimes in very subtle forms, the ideological concerns of neoliberalism. These, in turn, undermine other dimensions within religious traditions that offer resistance to such commodification, as seen, for example, in the Christian social gospel tradition of the nineteenth and twentieth centuries. The constant reinforcement of privatisation and individualism as conceptual spaces for thinking about 'the religious' restricts the very possibility of 'thinking differently' (Foucault, 1992: 9). In turn, academic discussions become ways of developing niche markets for professional academic egos rather than seeking to offer collective contributions to the wider society. Pointless internal debates, increased bureaucracy and a rhetoric of ongoing improvement and modernisation weaken the political resolve of the academic community and perpetuate the ideologies that increasingly govern the system. Such a system breaks academic projects into individualistic competitions where 'religion' and 'spirituality' can be abstractly cultivated by a new generation of consumers distracted from the social injustice that the packaging of these ideas continues to sanction. This does not mean that there is some real or authentic meaning to these terms waiting to be uncovered but rather that there is need to reflect upon the political site of scholarship and of the university as a site of intellectual resistance to offer alternative models of thinking that resist the neoliberal takeover of the subject. This will enable alternative readings and aspects of the traditions to be examined, which can then resist the terms set by the silent takeover.

In certain sectors of higher education, where the market demands for survival are the greatest, there is a tendency to compromise academic values and standards as a means of survival in a competitive and under-funded marketplace. In a capitalist system the subject of 'Religious Studies' provides a window to the exotic that allows 'knowledge-consumers' to 'buy-into' certain options, which either confirms their own normality and modernity or supports their need to feel counter-cultural and exotic. Religion becomes a commodity that is sold on the intellectual market like everything else. How does the teaching of religion in schools and universities reinforce the emergence of consumerist approaches to spirituality? First, by divorcing an understanding of religious beliefs from engagement with specific forms of life, the religions are rendered more amenable to detraditionalisation and distillation in terms of the modern concept of spirituality. Second, the modularisation of university courses encourages a 'pick and mix' approach to 'packaged' units of knowledge. Third, the 'world religions' paradigm that dominates educational approaches to religion encourages cultural stereotyping and the commodification of what are internally diverse and rich cultural traditions and institutions.

In the UK context of higher education, with its system of regular research quality assessments, teaching inspections and the language of 'transferable skills', learning outcomes and 'excellence', the effect of neoliberalism on the educational ethos is such that it hardly matters now *what* you teach or even *how* you teach it, as long as you can provide the appropriate documentation to demonstrate that your courses can be mapped in terms of supposedly generic and transferable skills, deemed necessary for a flexible workforce. The subject being studied becomes reduced to its utilitarian basics, and degrees become little more than training courses for 'tooling up' the workforce to meet the competitive demands of global capitalism. As Bill Readings (1996: 29) suggests,

> Is it surprising that corporations resemble Universities, health-care facilities, and international organizations, which all resemble corporations? . . . The notion of excellence, functioning less to permit visual observation than to permit exhaustive accounting, works to tie the University into a similar net of bureaucratic institutions. 'Excellence', that is, functions to allow the University to understand itself solely in terms of the structure of corporate administration.

This, of course, creates enormous tensions between the utilitarian ethos of management and the academics themselves, some of whom occasionally remain stubbornly committed to old-fashioned 'academic values' such as the pursuit of knowledge for its own sake, and the value of education for its intrinsic rather than narrowly utilitarian benefits. The renaming of 'Personnel' departments as 'Human Resources' in many organisations (not just higher education 'corporations') reflects an ideological shift that permeates into the very act of thinking or the numbing of thinking. Employees become 'resources' to be used, retrained, recycled or ultimately discarded. Students as a body of consumers become instrumentalist in assessing the outcomes and needs of their courses, and the value of subject content becomes diminished in terms of its market value. Education has become the machine of capitalism, and 'knowledge', as the British Prime Minister Tony Blair declared in a Labour Party conference speech, 'is human capital' (Labour Party Conference, October 2003). When knowledge becomes a form of 'capital' we begin to see how the language of the market is beginning to infiltrate all aspects of human life. When employees become 'human resources' – they too become forms of 'capital', which can be exchanged, exploited and retrained according to their utilitarian usefulness for the global economy. In this process the traditional distinction between (living) human and (inanimate) commodity begins to blur, and some humans become means rather than ends in themselves. Such is the new regime of thought-control in the modern neoliberal state. These subtle changes in language reflect underlying shifts in value-systems. They also demonstrate how ideas such as 'spirituality' can become instruments of a socio-political ideology that sees 'knowledge' as 'capital' and human beings as resources.

Within this shifting cultural context, the discipline of Religious Studies in effect becomes a self-indulgent intellectual *cul-de-sac*, maintaining the political ideology of neoliberalism, so long as its practitioners fail to recognise how 'religion' and 'spirituality' as concepts are being used in the service of largely hidden economic ideologies. Indeed the religion of the market is now increasingly acting as the dominant 'theology' through which the representations of the various 'religions' are filtered; and 'religious' ideas are being professionally produced by a new information proletariat, largely unaware of its collusion with the privatisation and corporatisation of the market. The danger, of course, is that the very act of resistance may itself be absorbed into the marketing machine, but to use the market to increase awareness of social injustice is at least the starting point of imagining different worlds from the one being presented to us as a *fait accompli*.

The neoliberal paradigm transforms a human employee (granted certain basic rights under liberalism) into an individualised 'human resource' who must be continually subjected to a regime of further training and behavioural correction through a series of in-house 'staff development' programmes designed to increase his or her efficiency, productivity and overall commitment to the company. Without such corrective measures, which often include short or fixed-term contracts, performance-related pay, and a general diminution of working conditions and employment and pension rights – all masked by a rhetoric of 'modernisation' – the employee would be considered unproductive and therefore liable for redundancy. Ironically, however, the corporate cult of efficiency in its own obsession with auditing and surveillance is itself inefficient. As

> '[W]e refuse to believe that the bank of justice is bankrupt.'
>
> Martin Luther King, Jr, 'I Have a Dream' speech, Washington, August 1963.

Tawney (1990: 283) notes in his classic study *Religion and the Rise of Capitalism*: 'Economic efficiency is a necessary element in the life of any sane and vigorous society . . . But to convert efficiency from an instrument into a primary object is to destroy efficiency itself.'

In the attempt to be more efficient, institutions set up committees to assess the functioning of the institution and, in so doing, take time away from the original purpose of the institution. In such a situation, it is vital that alternative models are found that can challenge the one-dimensional truth of the market. It is perhaps in recognising how 'the religions' might be re-engaged as a means of resisting consumerism and offering models of social justice that we can find ways to think differently about 'spirituality'. It is necessary to take the discourse of 'spirituality' out of the hands of consumerism, privatisation and corporate business and build a new locus of resistance that takes seriously the diverse cultural and civilisational roots of the modern world.

Conclusion

Engaged spiritualities can resist neoliberal forms of capitalism and the takeover of religion.

Consider three uses of the word 'religious' in relation to the contemporary world.

> The twenty-first century will be *religious*, or it will not be at all.
>
> (André Malraux)

> In the end, neoliberals cannot and do not offer an empirical defense for the world they are making. To the contrary, they offer – no, demand – *a religious faith* in the infallibility of the unregulated market that draws upon nineteenth-century theories that have little connection to the actual world. The ultimate trump card for the defenders of neoliberalism, however, is that there is no alternative.
>
> (Robert W. McChesney, 1999: 8)

> 'Modern capitalism' writes Mr Keynes, 'is absolutely *irreligious*, without internal union, without much public spirit, often, though not always, a mere congeries of possessors and pursuers.' It is that whole system of appetites and values, with its deification of the life of snatching to hoard, and hoarding to snatch, which now, in the hour of its triumph, while the plaudits of the crowd still ring in the ears of the gladiators and the laurels are still unfaded on their brows, seems sometimes to leave a taste as of ashes on the lips of a civilisation which has brought to the conquest of its material environment resources unknown in earlier ages, but which has not yet learned to master itself.
>
> (R. H. Tawney, [1922] 1990: 280)

In two of the above quotations we see modern capitalism described both as 'a religious faith' and as 'irreligious'. Both McChesney and

Tawney use the word religion to make an ethical appeal, but one sees religion negatively as dogmatic and disconnected from worldly realities (McChesney) and the other sees religion as the provider of a positive sense of social ethics (Tawney). It is perhaps the apocryphal quotation by Malraux, that the twenty-first century will be 'religious' or it will not be at all, that is the most appropriate of the three. 'Religion' is a contested site, but one that holds centuries of rich association and power; it evokes positive and negative images, it is constantly reimagined and reinvented and provides a wealth of ideas for assertions of power. Religious ideas, like it or not, shape the cultural imagination and have the power to inspire people not only to make money and kill others (the violent and exploitative aspects of religion) but also to stand and fight for justice and build societies which care for the weakest (the social justice elements of religion). This is the conceptual territory of religion, and 'spirituality' is one of its frontiers.

In the course of this book we have sought to show how the idea of 'spirituality' has been through two stages of privatisation: first, individualisation, through a process of psycho-political normalisation, and second, corporatisation, through the processes of neoliberalism. The result of this cultural organisation of the term 'spirituality' in the late twentieth and early twenty-first centuries is a support for the ideologies of consumerism and corporate capitalism. It reflects the silent takeover of all aspects of life by the corporate world and the interests of capital. The very conceptual spaces of contemporary life have become ideologically soaked in the language and ideology of the market. Neoliberal ideology seeps into the very fabric of how we think, indeed into the very possibilities of our thinking to such an extent that people now live as if the corporate capitalist structures of our world are the truth of our existence. Capital determines thought, like Newspeak in Orwell's *Nineteen Eighty-Four*, and the very act of thinking *otherwise* becomes ever more difficult.

> The purpose of Newspeak was not only to provide a medium of
> expression for the worldview and mental habits proper to the devotee
> of Ingsoc, but to make all other modes of thought impossible. It was

intended that when Newspeak had been adopted once and for all and
Oldspeak forgotten, a heretical thought – that is a thought diverging
from the principles of Ingsoc – should be literally unthinkable, at least
so far as thought is dependent on words.

(Orwell, 1989: 312)

In this book we have seen how 'religion' has been repackaged and
commodified for consumption through the idea of 'spirituality' and
we have seen how business has used the positive gloss of 'spirituality'
to support its corporate interests and working practices. The attempt
to model social life in its totality upon the ideologies and practices
of the market directs the search for meaning and value towards the
rather limited perspective of their instrumental and monetary value.
However, as Confucius reminds us, the superior mind understands
moral goodness, while the inferior understands only profit (*Analects*,
IV.16).

'Spirituality,' of course, refers to a wide range of phenomena
and can carry a variety of different meanings. Modern forms of
spirituality, as well as the ancient traditions that they draw upon for
inspiration, need not be read in narrowly individualistic or capitalist
forms. Indeed, our aim within this book has been to contest such
readings of the wisdom of our various world religions. We have
sought to open up a space for critical reflection upon some of
the prevailing tendencies within contemporary discourses of 'the
spiritual' by considering the ideologies that they tend to support. This
project is not motivated, as some who may misread our work might
assume, in order to appeal to some privileged space of ancient
religious authenticity, some nodal point where 'true religion' or 'true
spirituality' might be found – for this has not been our concern.
Nevertheless, in challenging the colonisation of our collective cultural
heritage by individualist and capitalist forms of spirituality, we have
inevitably emphasised what they have silenced within those traditions,
namely a concern with community, social justice and the extension of
an ethical ideal of selfless love and compassion towards others.

The market analysts are correct, however, to suggest that ideas can
change lives. In the attempt to resist the privatisation of 'spirituality',

in both its individualist and its corporatist forms, we seek to support alternative models of 'spirituality' that pay attention to the politics of knowledge, community and questions of social justice. The use of an idea such as 'spirituality' is *always* bound up with political questions, even when the term is defined in apparently apolitical terms (in which case it supports the status quo). In employing the word, it is important to identify which ideological concerns are being supported. Like the French thinker Michel Foucault, we intend our work to be read *strategically* as a critical response to a dominant ideological configuration. Thinking, according to Foucault, is like Judo ('the way of yielding', originally a Taoist martial art). You make a move strategically and then wait for the next assertion of power. It is not possible to appeal to some immutable and universal meaning of terms like 'spirituality' or 'religion' (for instance, in arguing that 'real spirituality' is socially engaged) because meanings change over time and take on new resonances according to shifting power-relations within society. One important move Foucault made, however, was to draw attention to the history of power-relations involved in the construction of meanings. By raising an awareness of the forgotten and silenced aspects of traditions one is able to offer counter-readings of dominant discourses.

We seek then to support a counter-discourse, grounded in an emphasis upon social justice and compassion, in order to displace the privatised and neo-liberal framing of 'spirituality'. In so doing, we are seeking to align ourselves explicitly with socially engaged trends within the contested domain of 'spirituality' and offer a corrective to the dominant trends that have emerged within the 'Mind, Body, Spirit' sphere. In order to do this, however, one must

> 'All my books . . . are little tool boxes . . . [I]f people want to open them to use this sentence or that idea as a screwdriver or spanner to short-circuit, discredit or smash systems of power, including eventually those from which my books have emerged . . . so much the better.'
>
> Cited in Paul Patton, 'Of Power and Prisons', in Meaghan Morris and Paul Patton (eds), *Michel Foucault: Power/Truth/Strategy*, Feral Productions, 1979, p. 115.

first raise awareness of the implications of uncritically using terms such as 'spirituality'. In a contemporary western context the concept is most likely to be interpreted as referring to a privatised, individualistic and largely 'post-religious' phenomenon. One of our key aims within this work has been to identify some of the dominant trends in this use of the term at the beginning of the twenty-first century and shed some light upon the political structures such usage supports and reflects. By offering what one might call an *anti-capitalist* (or better, *alter-mondialiste*) reading of 'spirituality' we are aligning ourselves explicitly with a variety of socially engaged movements that provide evidence of a radically different reading of the concept.

CAPITALISM – THE NEW GLOBAL RELIGION?

There have always been intimate links between religious traditions and local economies. What we call 'the religions' remain embedded in worldly institutions and social practices. Such interactions between 'the religious' and 'the economic' have been varied in their

> 'Beneath the lofty aims of the corporate spirituality movement lives capitalism's enduring need to maximize labor's output at the lowest possible cost.'
>
> Budde and Brinlow 2002: 34

nature, not least because in a pre-modern context the 'economic' and the 'religious' were never sharply differentiated realms. Indeed it is only in the modern era that economic theory and practice has become divorced from the social and treated as an autonomous realm. However, at the end of the twentieth century with the collapse of the Soviet Union, we have seen the emergence of free market economics (neoliberalism) as the new orthodoxy of our times. As Harvey Cox (1999: 20) has pointed out:

> Since the earliest stages of human history, of course, there have been bazaars, rialtos and trading posts – all markets. But The Market was never God, because there were other centers of value and meaning, other 'gods'. The Market operated within a plethora of other institutions that restrained it. As Karl Polanyi has demonstrated in his classic work *The Great Transformation*, only in the past two centuries has The Market risen above these demigods and chthonic spirits to become today's First Cause.

The development of a globalised and finance-based capitalist system is challenging the sovereignty of the nation-state and its ability to control economic transactions across its borders. No longer held in check by other countervailing forces in society (such as the ideals of individual restraint, a social conscience and the promotion of a community-oriented ethic by traditional religious institutions), Capitalism has become the new religion of the contemporary (postmodern) world. As the Buddhist scholar David Loy (2002: 200) suggests in his discussion of contemporary western culture,

> If we are not blinded by the distinction usually made between secular and sacred, we can see that advertising promises another kind of salvation, i.e., another way to solve our lack. Insofar as this strikes at the heart of the truly religious perspective – which offers an alternative explanation for our inability to be happy and a very different path to become happy – religions are not fulfilling their responsibility if they ignore this religious dimension of capitalism, if they do not emphasise that this seduction is deceptive because this solution to our unhappiness leads only to greater dissatisfaction.

As with the rise of religious ideologies in previous historical eras, 'the Market' is being presented to us as 'natural' and inevitable (rather than contingent and socially constructed). It is gradually infiltrating all other dimensions of human life, translating and transforming everything in its wake into the language and philosophy of consumerism – a world of competitiveness, economically driven motivation and de-regulated market forces. Rather than setting out to convert the heathen to the gospel, as generations of European Christians did, or bring civilisation to the primitive, as their Enlightenment successors sought to achieve, the explicit goal in this new phase of missionary activity is to convert the people of the world into consumers and all human societies into deregulated markets. To achieve this task requires the transformation or outright removal of traditional institutions and modes of authority within those societies under the banner of modernisation and their replacement by new institutional forms and policies explicitly designed to bring about the active transformation of the consciousnesses of human beings. This missionary project is to be carried out through the mass media and educational institutions and by the power of advertising in order to create new desires for the latest consumer products.

In this way, bombarded by media images of western affluence and celebrity endorsements of the 'virtues' of this product or that, in a seemingly endless cycle of consumption, more and more aspects of our lives are presented to us in the language of the marketplace. Life becomes a series of choices between competing brand-names and privatised (rather than state-organised) social services. Students and hospital patients become consumers, rail passengers become customers, politicians become 'spin-doctors' promoting their own particular brand of bland managerialism, and religious ideas and practices become commodities for sale to alleviate the angst of the modern, isolated individual. The theology underlying this trans- formation of our thought processes in the late twentieth century is neoliberalism. The marketisation of more and more features of human life and culture, that the spread of neoliberalism is creating within societies, has reached such heights (or perhaps depths), that we can now legitimately (that is, in *legal* terms) talk of the commodification of life itself. With the patenting of human genes by multinational companies and the emergence of intellectual copyright laws that seek to maintain restrictions upon the ownership of ideas ('intellectual capital'), everything has its price, but nothing maintains its value. This presents an unprecedented challenge not only to society and to the world as a whole but also to traditional religions and the emerging discourse of 'spirituality' that is accompanying this transformation.

We are under no illusions that, historically, the traditional religions have been sources of social oppression as well as grounding ethical sensibilities about compassion and social justice. Ken Wilber, a well-known author within the 'spirituality' literature we have been exploring, has argued that all religions have a 'translative' and a 'trans- formative' dimension. The former, he suggests, corresponds to most of what a religious tradition in practice relates to, and involves institutional and social means for meeting the everyday needs of human beings, that is, in providing ways for people to accommodate themselves to the world in which they live. It is this aspect of the religious that particularly preoccupied Marx and other secular critics of religion because it was seen as providing, in the famous phrase, 'an opiate for the masses', preventing a full realisation of worker alienation under capitalism and therefore a bulwark against social revolution on the part of the oppressed proletarian masses. Wilber, however, like many advocates of 'the religious life' before him, argues that there is another dimension to the religious – one that is revolutionary in its potentiality and unsettling of the status quo rather than accommodationist. Wilber admits that this has generally been the preserve of a small elite within each tradition, but it has also tended to represent the highest ideals of that tradition – inspiring humans to transcend their own individual concerns and petty desires and to see the bigger picture. While it is not always clear what socially trans-formative aspects result from Wilber's own brand of 'transpersonal spirituality', it is certainly this more exalted dimension of the religions that most people have in mind when they make the contemporary distinction between 'spirituality' (seen as a holistic, non-dogmatic and wholesome, *good* thing) and 'religion' (seen as an outdated, con-flict-causing and ritualistic, *bad* thing).

A hard-and-fast distinction between the transformative and accommodationist aspects of the religious is highly problematic, not least because these can radically vary according to context. Neverthe-less, it does represent a dichotomy that has become more and more popular within western societies. This can be seen in the increasing tendency for the term 'spirituality' to displace 'religion' as the pre-ferred designation for those wishing to embrace what they see as the 'positive' aspects of the religious that should be retained while rejecting its traditional, institutional forms as some kind of dis-pensable 'outer husk'. Ironically, the emergence of the contemporary concept of 'spirituality' as 'post-religious' may prove useful in re-engaging with the transformative and revolutionary capacity of traditional religious teachings in a way that obviates Marx's basic criticism of the religions as modes of social control. In a context where 'the Market' has become the new God of our times (Cox, 1999), the emergence of socially oriented forms of 'spirituality', critically engaging with the wisdom of the world's 'religious' tradi-tions, may yet have a key role to play in providing the means for resisting unrestrained consumerism and the commodification of life itself.

SPIRITUALITY AND CAPITALISM: RESISTANCE IS NOT FUTILE

The anti-capitalist movement embraces a variety of different political perspectives and a commitment to unity in diversity is one of its most strongly affirmed – and widely practised – organizing principles. This is *an* anti-capitalist manifesto: there can and should be many others.

(Callinicos, 2003: 20)

After the collapse of Communism and Marxism, there is a vacuum in framing an ideological resistance to global capitalism, which in the 1990s has been triumphalist in its celebration of the end of history (Fukuyama). What has been called the 'anti-capitalist movement' (or in French *alter-mondialiste*, reflecting the internationalist focus of most groups) is an emerging network of intellectual positions and diverse social movements, which lacks coherence. This is both its strength and its weakness. However, if the movement is to mobilise support it will need to be clearer about its objectives and what it stands for. It is important to recognise for instance that the historical roots of the traditions of social justice and criticism that find a voice in the anti-capitalist movement are themselves grown in the soil of the various religious traditions of the world.

We would argue that in order for the anti-capitalist movement to articulate its opposition to global capitalism and the ideology of consumerism on a global scale, it must challenge the secular confines of its own social critique (established in modern European thought by figures such as Feuerbach, Marx and Nietzsche). The most effective way to do this and to extend such reflection beyond a narrowly Eurocentric perspective is to engage with the intellectual and moral reflections of the world's intellectual/religious traditions. Most of the people on this planet understand the significance of their lives and the world as a whole through the mediating lenses of these great traditions. They have not experienced 'the death of God' that so many secular theorists and political activists in the West have proclaimed. One cannot expect an international coalition of resistance to corporate capitalism and the commodification of existence to capture the hearts and minds of the multitude, unless it acknowledges their own indigenous worldviews and forms of life. It is precisely this global diversity which the Seattle Consensus of anti-capitalist movements and movements such as the Zapatistas of Chiapas in Mexico, are seeking to preserve. Moreover, for the vast majority of the world's population, a 'secular' ideology that de-sacralises the world far too easily ends up turning it into a commodity. This suggests that avowedly secular ideologies may be part of the problem rather than the solution.

What of the response from the religious traditions themselves? As worldly institutions populated by human beings like the rest of us, the various religious traditions and movements have largely evolved through a series of compromises and reconfigurations to a position of accommodating capitalism and consumerism as ways of life. It has not generally been acknowledged that such traditions are becoming subject to a takeover precisely because members of these traditions have failed to see the increasingly *religious* quality of capitalism in the modern world.

The corporatisation of the world's cultural and religious traditions commodifies human cultural heritage and subordinates its concerns to the economic theology of neoliberalism. This theology takes its values from corporate capitalism – the new religion of the Market. Its God is 'Capital' and its ethics highly questionable. This leaves those with an interest in the traditional 'space of the religious' with a choice to make. They can allow themselves and their traditions to be co-opted by and assimilated into this new religious ideology as accommodationist spiritualities offering succour and relief to an alienated and dehumanised congregation of individualised consumers. This, after all, has been the fate of most of the religions of the past, to have their gods, rituals and practices taken over and rebranded by the new religion in town. Ultimately, of course, this means the death of that tradition, or at least the end of life in and on its own terms. We can see this, for instance, if we consider the ways in which the 'pagan' celebration of Yuletide has been transformed. First, taken over by the Christians it became Christmas – the celebration of the birth of the Christian saviour, and now commodified and taken over by the religion of capitalism, it is a festival celebrating the excesses of consumerism. Even the red dress code of 'Santa Claus' is itself the result of an early 'branding' of the concept by the Coca Cola Company in the 1930s, a fact often forgotten when the image is used.

A second option for the religions is to retreat into a siege mentality and pray that the predicted Armageddon will not happen. Again, the history of such strategies suggests that this is simply deferring one's own demise. A third option is to challenge this process, which is only inevitable if we allow it to be, and recapture the discursive space of 'the spiritual' as a site of resistance. This in effect is an alternative 'rebranding' of the religions of the past – this time as the *'atheistic heresies' and liberationist discourses of the twenty-first century*. They are atheistic in the sense articulated by Argentinian philosopher/liberation theologian Enrique Dussel, namely, that they reject mainstream belief in the God of Capital, and liberationist in the sense that they put social justice before private profit.

If capitalism is indeed the new triumphant ideology of our times and Marxism its apparently defeated heresy, what we need at this moment in history are new 'atheisms' that reject the God of money. In the brave new world of the twenty-first century those perspectives that are classified as 'religious' in the modern consciousness provide the best

> 'Compromise is as impossible between the Church of Christ and the idolatry of wealth, which is the practical religion of capitalist societies, as it was between the Church and the State idolatry of the Roman Empire.'
>
> R. H. Tawney, *Religion and the Rise of Capitalism: A Historical Study*, 1926, p. 286.

hope we have as philosophical, social and cultural resources for this struggle. The 'religions', old and new, are, in fact, the potential atheisms of the present age. What a supreme irony indeed if we come to realise that the significance of Nietzsche and Marx's critique of the 'opiate of the masses' is that it is the religions themselves that provide the best hope for humanity in challenging the God of Money and providing the basic foundations on which to build alternative ideologies to the dominant religion of the early twenty-first century – corporate capitalism.

In arguing for the importance of those traditions designated as 'the religions' in the modern world, we are certainly not taking a traditionalist view that would argue for a return to old-time religions and orthodoxies. Resistance must always be open to new discursive formations of 'the spiritual' and the rise of new social movements and traditions. Indeed, as we have seen, contemporary uses of the term 'spirituality' range across the traditional 'secular' and 'religious' divide. You can be 'spiritual' nowadays without necessarily aligning with a particular religious tradition. As we have seen, this is over-whelmingly because the dominant discourse of 'spirituality' is grounded in the modern capitalist ideology of individualism. This fluidity across secular and religious boundaries has been one factor in the usefulness of the concept for the corporate takeover. This same feature of the term, however, also provides the possibility of new configurations of resistance – in terms that are not blinded by the modernist separation of the religious from the secular.

Since assertions of power always create the conditions for their own resistance, we should expect to see a number of movements arise in the twenty-first century that cannot easily be classified as either 'secularist' or 'religious' in the modern (Enlightenment) sense of these terms. There are numerous examples of such movements in the contemporary world. They include Third-World liberation theologies (articulating a Christian concern for the poor and the disadvantaged), the Zapatistas (reflecting an indigenous but very contemporary blend of Mayan and Catholic traditions in direct confrontation with neo-liberalism), the 'tree-hugging' Chipko movement of the Himalayas (grounded in Gandhian-inspired social resistance and ecological concern), the Swadhyaya movement for social upliftment in western India (developing a model of social justice and redistribution based upon the teachings of the Hindu Vedanta traditions), the various forms of Socially Engaged Buddhism (such as Thich Nhat Hanh's Order of Interbeing and the Ambedhkarites) rooting their critique of social injustice in Buddhist principles, to name but a few. All represent new social movements that are borne out of a fertile engagement between traditional indigenous perspectives and civilisations and contemporary socio-political concerns.

The dichotomy between the secular and the religious, so central to the western project of modernity and liberalism, may well be in the process of unravelling. Neoliberalism is one of the products of this cultural and political shift, as is the increasingly religious appearance of capitalism. This is why to follow Karl Marx's critique in the contemporary world we must *go beyond* Marx. When global terrorism *and* global capitalism both exploit religious language, traditions and allegiances to make their case – most notably, in the case of the West, with its notions of a crusade, of 'freedom' and of 'the civilised world' – it is imperative that we reclaim the ground of social justice from the fundamentalists – whether they be of the Islamic, Christian, secularist or 'free-market' persuasion – and prevent them from setting the terms of the debate. We should be rightly suspicious of calls for a return to the religious traditions of the past; and, in any case, there can be no going back. These same traditions, however, should attract our respect as well as our criticism, for they have also moulded our civilisations, our sense of ethics and community and our concern for social justice. As Robert Bocock (1993: 119) has argued,

> The world's religions are an important resource of moral values, of caring orientations towards nature, and for providing a critique of capitalist consumption patterns if they can be disengaged from ethnic groups' rivalries for territory. The world's religions remain in contact with millions of ordinary people in the world, unlike the atheistic positivism derived from the Enlightenment of some Western intellectuals and some materialist communists. The world's religions could help in overcoming the ideology of consumerism, and the social-economic practices associated with consumption, before the damage to the planet is too great to sustain 'civilised' forms of living.

Emerging as it did out of the complex processes associated with secularisation and 'the disenchantment of the world' (Weber) in Northern European societies, unfettered capitalism results in the de-sacralisation of life. Like the *Borg*, the marauding alien race in the US TV franchise *Star Trek*, capitalism without restraint turns everything it encounters into a commodity to be assimilated and used or thrown away. 'You will be assimilated,' the Borg tell us, 'Resistance is futile.' But resistance is not futile, and as the Mexican Zapatistas have said in response to the neoliberal challenge: 'Enough is Enough.'

Whether one wishes to tear down the structures of capitalism or simply limit the impact of an unrestrained market on societies and communities, one cannot expect to develop an ideological challenge to neoliberalism by constructing a similarly materialistic and economically oriented heresy – that is by appealing to a worldview that also accepts 'the disenchantment of the world'. Nor is an appeal to some vague and abstract global spirituality (Cousins, 1987; Korten, 1996: 325–8; Greider, 1997: 469) likely to succeed in speaking to indigenous peoples around the world who 'draw from the strength of their local traditions, not from the abstract values of universal theories' (Majid, 2000: 145). In the context of the dominance of the materialist ideology of capitalism in modern western societies, what we need today are 'spiritual atheisms' for our time, and the world's religious traditions provide the richest intellectual examples we have of humanity's collective effort to make sense of life, community and ethics. The emergence of new forms of engaged spirituality grounded in an awareness of our mutual interdependence, the need for social justice and economically sustainable lifestyles, may yet prove our best hope for resisting the capitalist excesses of neoliberalism and developing a sense of solidarity and global citizenship in an increasingly precarious world. Our futures may depend upon it.

References

Addiss, Stephen, and Stanley Lombardo, 1993, *The Tao Te Ching*, Hackett.

Allport, Gordon, [1950] 1962, *The Individual and His Religion*, Macmillan.

Almond, Philip, 1988, *The British Discovery of Buddhism*, Cambridge University Press.

Badiner, Allen (ed.), 2002, *Mindfulness in the Marketplace: Compassionate Responses to Consumerism*, Parallax Press.

Bagot, Laurence, 2003, 'Alpharetta L'illuminée', *Enjeux Les Echos* 193 (July–August): 46–9.

Batchelor, Stephen, 1997, *Buddhism Without Beliefs*, Putnam.

Baumann, Zygmunt, 1998, 'Postmodern Religion', in Paul Heelas, David Martin and Paul Morris (eds), *Religion, Modernity and Postmodernity*, Blackwells.

Beaudoin, Tom, 2003, *Consuming Faith: Integrating Who We Are with What We Buy*, Sheed & Ward.

Beck, Clive, 1986, 'Education for Spirituality', *Interchange* 17: 148–56.

Bell, Daniel, 1979, *The Cultural Contradictions of Capitalism*, Heinemann.

Bellah, Robert N., Richard Madsen, William M. Sullivan, Ann Swidler and Steven M. Tipton, 1985, *Habits of the Heart: Individualism and Commitment in American Life*, University of California Press.

Benn, Tony, 2002, *An Audience with Tony Benn*, Hodder Headline Audiobooks.

Blackman, Lisa (ed.), 2003, *Spirituality: International Journal of Critical Psychology* Issue 8.

Bobbitt, Philip, 2002, *The Shield of Achilles: War, Peace and the Course of History*, Penguin.

Bocock, Robert, 1993, *Consumption*, Routledge.

Boyle, David, 2001, *The Tyranny of Numbers: Why Counting Can't Make Us Happy*, Flamingo.

Brazier, David, 2001, *The New Buddhism*, Palgrave-Macmillan.

Bridle, Susan, 2001, 'The Man with the Golden Tongue', in *The Modern Spiritual Predicament: An Inquiry in the Popularization of East-Meets-West Spirituality*, Issue 12 of *What Is Enlightenment* (March).

Browning, Don, 1987, *Religious Thought and Modern Psychologies*, Fortress Press.

Bruneau, Marie-Florine, 1998, *Women Mystics Confront the Modern World*, State University of New York Press.

Budde, Michael and Brinlow, Robert, 2002, *Christianity Incorporated. How Big Business is Buying the Church*, Brazos Press.

Callinicos, Alex, 2003, *An Anti-Capitalist Manifesto*, Polity Press.

Carayol, Rene, and David Firth, 2001, *Corporate Voodoo: Principles for Business Mavericks and Magicians*, Capstone.

Carrette, Jeremy, 2000, *Foucault and Religion*, Routledge.

Carrette, Jeremy, 2001, 'Post-Structuralism and the Psychology of Religion: The Challenge of Critical Psychology', in Diane Jonte-Pace and William Parsons (eds), Religion and Psychology: Mapping the Terrain, Routledge.

Carrette, Jeremy, 2003, 'Psychology, Spirituality and Capitalism: The Case of Abraham Maslow', in Lisa Blackman (ed.), Spirituality: International Journal of Critical Psychology Issue 8: 73–95.

Carroll, Lewis, [1907] 1948, Alice's Adventures in Wonderland, Heinemann.

Carroll, Lewis, [1871] 1994, Through the Looking Glass and What Alice Found Here, Penguin Classic.

Chomsky, Noam, 1989, Necessary Illusions: Thought Control in Democratic Societies, South End Press.

Chomsky, Noam, 1999, Profit Over People: Neoliberalism and Global Order, Seven Stories Press.

Chopra, Deepak, 1993, Ageless Body, Timeless Mind, Crown Books.

Clarke, J. J., 1997, Oriental Enlightenment: The Encounter Between Asian and Western Thought, Routledge.

Clarke, J. J., 2000, The Tao of the West: Taoism in Western Thought, Routledge.

Conze, Edward, I. B. Horner, David Snellgrove and Arthur Waley (eds), 1964, Buddhist Texts Through the Ages, Harper Torchbooks.

Cousins, Ewert, 1987, 'Spirituality in Today's World', in Frank Whaling (ed.), Religion in Today's World, T&T Clark.

Cox, Harvey, 1977, Turning East: The Promise and Peril of the New Orientalism, Simon & Schuster.

Cox, Harvey, 1999, 'The Market as God', The Atlantic (March): 18–23.

Cox, Harvey, 2003, 'Christianity', in Mark Juergensmeyer (ed.), Global Religions: An Introduction, Oxford University Press.

Crosby, Kate, and Andrew Skilton, 1996, The Bodhicaryavatara, Oxford University Press.

Emmons, Robert, 1999, The Psychology of Ultimate Concerns: Motivations and Spirituality in Personality, Guilford Press.

Estruch, Joan, 1996, Saints and Schemers: Opus Dei and its Paradoxes, Oxford University Press.

Fevre, R. W., 2000, The Demoralisation of Western Culture, Continuum.

Fitzgerald, Timothy, 2000, The Ideology of Religious Studies, Oxford University Press.

Foucault, Michel, 1980, Power/Knowledge: Selected Interviews and Other Writings 1972–1977, Harvester Wheatsheaf.

Foucault, Michel, 1982, 'The Subject and Power', in Michel Foucault: Beyond Structuralism and Hermeneutics, Harvester Wheatsheaf.

Foucault, Michel, [1984] 1992, The Use of Pleasure, Penguin.

Fox, Judith, 2002, Osho Rajneesh, Signature Books.

Friedman, Thomas, 2000, The Lexus and the Olive Tree, Anchor Books/Doubleday.

Fromm, Erich, [1978] 1950, Psychoanalysis and Religion, Yale University Press.

Fromm, Erich, [1970] 1995, 'Problems of Surplus', in The Essential Fromm, Constable.

Fromm, Erich, 2004, *The Dogma of Christ and Other Essays on Religion, Psychology and Culture*, Routledge Classics.

Fukuyama, M. A., and T. Sevig, 1999, *Integrating Spirituality into Multicultural Counselling*, Sage.

Gilliat-Ray, Sophie, 2003, 'Nursing, Professionalism, and Spirituality', *Journal of Contemporary Religion* 18(3): 335–49.

Goodchild, Philip, 2002, *Capitalism and Religion: The Price of Piety*, Routledge.

Grant, John, 2000, *The New Marketing Manifesto: The 12 Rules for Building Successful Brands in the 21st Century*, Texere.

Greider, William, 1997, *One World, Ready or Not: The Manic Logic of Global Capitalism*, Simon & Schuster.

Hansen, Susan, Alex McHol and Mark Rapley, 2003, *Beyond Help: A Consumer's Guide to Psychology*, PCCS.

Heelas, Paul, 1996, *The New Age Movement*, Blackwells.

Hertz, Noreena, 2001, *The Silent Takeover: Global Capitalism and the Death of Democracy*, William Heinemann.

Ignatius of Loyola, 1914, *The Spiritual Exercises*, translated from the Autograph by Father Elder Mullan, SJ, IHS, P. J. Kennedy & Sons.

James, William, [1902] 2002, *The Varieties of Religious Experience*, Centenary Edition, Routledge.

Jantzen, Grace, 1995, *Power, Gender and Christian Mysticism*, Cambridge University Press.

Jones, Laurie Beth, 1995, *Jesus, CEO: Using Ancient Wisdom for Visionary Leadership*, Hyperion.

Julian, Larry, 2001, *God is My CEO: Following God's Principles in a Bottom-Line World*, Adams Media Corporation.

Jung, C. G., [1932] 1958, 'Psychotherapists or Clergy', in *Psychology and Religion: West and East*, C. G. Jung's Collected Works, vol. 11, Routledge & Kegan Paul.

Jung, C. G., [1933] 1984, *Modern Man in Search of A Soul*, Routledge & Kegan Paul.

King, Richard, 1995, *Early Advaita Vedanta and Buddhism: The Mahayana Context of the Gaudapadiyakarika*, State University of New York Press.

King, Richard, 1999a, *Orientalism and Religion: Postcolonial Theory, India and 'the Mystic East'*, Routledge.

King, Richard, 1999b, *Indian Philosophy: An Introduction to Hindu and Buddhist Thought*, Edinburgh University Press and Georgetown University Press.

King, Sallie B., and Christopher Queen (eds), 1996, *Engaged Buddhism: Buddhist Liberation Movements in Asia*, State University of New York Press.

Klein, Naomi, 2001, *No Logo*, Flamingo.

Klein, Naomi, 2002, 'America Is Not a Hamburger', *Los Angeles Times*, 10 March, reprinted in Naomi Klein, *Fences and Windows: Dispatches from the Front Lines of the Globalization Debate*, Flamingo, 2002.

Korten, David, 1996, *When Corporations Rule the World*, Kumarian Press and Berrett-Koehler.

Koslowski, Rey, and Friedrich Kratochwil, 1994, 'Understanding Change in

International Politics: The Soviet Empire's Demise and the International System', *International Organisations* 48 (Spring).

Kunde, Jesper, 2000, *Corporate Religion*, Prentice Hall.

Lambourn, David, 1996, ' "Spiritual" Minus "Personal-Social" = ?: A Critical Note on an "Empty" category', in Ron Best (ed.), *Education, Spirituality, and the Whole Child*, Cassell.

Lamont, Georgeanne, 2002, *The Spirited Business*, Hodder & Stoughton.

Lasch, Christopher, 1980, *The Culture of Narcisissm: American Life in an Age of Diminishing Expectation*, Abacus Press.

Lau, Kimberley J., 2000, *New Age Capitalism: Making Money East of Eden*, University of Pennsylvania Press.

Lee, Helen, 2001, 'Towards a Critical Politics of Spirituality', *Critical Psychology* 1: 153–7.

Lee, Helen, and Harriette Marshall, 2003, 'Divine Individualism: Transcending Psychology', in Lisa Blackman (ed.), *Spirituality: International Journal of Critical Psychology* Issue 8: 13–33.

Lee, Raymond M., 2003, 'The Re-enchantment of the Self: Western Spirituality, Asian Materialism', *Journal of Contemporary Religion* 18(3): 351–67.

Lopez, Jr, Donald, 1998, *Prisoners of Shangri La: Tibetan Buddhism and the West*, Chicago University Press.

Loy, David, 2002, *A Buddhist History of the West: Studies in Lack*, State University of New York Press.

Loy, David, 2003, *The Great Awakening: A Buddhist Social Theory*, Wisdom Publications.

McChesney, Robert W., 1999, 'Introduction', in Noam Chomsky, *Profit Over People: Neoliberalism and Global Order*, Seven Stories Press.

McKean, Lisa, 1996, *Divine Enterprise: Gurus and the Hindu Nationalist Movement*, University of Chicago Press.

Maduro, Otto, 1977, 'New Marxist Approaches to the Relative Autonomy of Religion', *Sociological Analysis* 38(4): 359–67.

Majid, Anouar, 2000, *Unveiling Traditions: Postcolonial Islam in a Polycentric World*, Duke University Press.

Maslow, Abraham, [1964] 1976, *Religions, Values and Peak-Experiences*, Penguin.

Michelis, Elizabeth de, 2004, *A History of Modern Yoga: Patañjali and Western Esotericism*, Continuum.

Miller, William R., and Carl E. Thoresen, 1999, 'Spirituality and Health', in William Miller (ed.), *Integrating Spirituality into Treatment*, American Psychological Association.

Negri, Antonio, and Michael Hardt, 2000, *Empire*, Harvard University Press.

Orwell, George, [1949] 1989, *Nineteen Eighty-Four*, Penguin.

Parker, Ian, 1997, *Psychoanalytic Culture*, Sage.

Payutto, Phra, 1995, *Buddhist Economics*, Buddhadhamma Foundation.

Peck, M. Scott, [1978] 1990, *The Road Less Travelled*, Arrow.

Pickering, W. S. F., 1975, *Durkheim on Religion: A Selection of Readings and Bibliographies*, Routledge & Kegan Paul.

Prashad, Vijay, 2000, The Karma of Brown Folk, University of Minnesota Press.

Principe, Walter, 1983, 'Toward Defining Spirituality', Sciences Religieuses/Studies in Religion 12: 127–41.

Queen, Christopher, 2000, Engaged Buddhism in the West, Wisdom Publications.

Queen, Christopher, Charles Prebish and Damien Keown (eds), 2003, Action Dharma: New Studies in Engaged Buddhism, Routledge/Curzon.

Readings, Bill, 1996, The University in Ruins, Harvard University Press.

Richards, Graham, 2002, Putting Psychology in its Place: A Critical Historical Overview, 2nd edn, Routledge.

Roberts, Richard, 2002, Religion, Theology and the Human Sciences, Cambridge University Press.

Roof, Wade Clarke, 1999, Spiritual Marketplace, Princeton University Press.

Roof, Wade Clarke, and Lyn Gesch, 1995, 'Boomers and the Culture of Choice: Changing Patterns of Work, Family and Religion in Contemporary America', in N. Ammerman and Wade Clarke Roof (eds), Work, Family and Religion in Contemporary America, Routledge.

Rose, Nikolas, 1990, Governing the Soul: The Shaping of the Private Self, Routledge.

Rose, Nikolas, 1998, Inventing Our Selves: Psychology, Power and Personhood, Cambridge University Press.

Rowe, Dorothy, 2001, 'What Do You Mean by Spiritual?' in Simon King-Spooner and Craig Newnes (eds), Spirituality and Psychotherapy, PCCS.

Russell, Stephen, 2002, Liberation: The Perfect Holistic Antidote to Stress, Depression and other Unhealthy States of Mind, HarperCollins.

Scanlon, Joyce, and Ann McLaughlin, 'Marketing Your Mind, Body, Spirit Business', http://www.ofspirit.com/annmclaughlin1.htm

Sivaraksa, Sulak, 2002, 'Alternatives to Consumerism', in A. Badiner (ed.), Mindfulness in the Marketplace, Parallax Press.

Sizemore, Russell, and Donald Swearer, 1993, Ethics, Wealth and Salvation: A Study in Buddhist Social Ethics, University of South Carolina Press.

Sklair, Leslie, 2002, Globalization. Capitalism and Its Alternatives, 3rd edn, Oxford University Press.

Sloan, Todd (ed.), 2000, Critical Psychology: Voices for Change, Sage.

Smail, David, [1987] 1998, Taking Care: An Alternative to Therapy, Constable.

Stanczak, G. C., and D. E. Miller, 2002, Engaged Spirituality: Spirituality and Social Transformation in Mainstream American Religious Traditions, Center for Religion and Civic Culture, University of Southern California.

Stephens, Deborah C. (ed.), 2000, The Maslow Business Reader, John Wiley & Sons.

Sutich, Anthony, 1969, 'Transpersonal Psychology: An Emerging Force', Journal of Humanistic Psychology 8(1): 77–8.

Swinton, John, 2001, Spirituality and Mental Health Care, Jessica Kingsley.

Tawney, R. H., [1922] 1990, Religion and the Rise of Capitalism: A Historical Study, Penguin.

Thrift, Nigel, 1997, 'Soft Capitalism', *Cultural Values* 1(2): 29–57.

Thurman, Robert, 1991, *The Holy Teachings of Vimalakirti: A Mahayana Scripture*, Motilal Banarsidass.

Tonigan, J. Scott, Radha T. Toscova, and Gerard J. Conners, 1999, 'Spirituality and the 12-Step Programs: A Guide for Clinicians', in William Miller (ed.), *Integrating Spirituality into Treatment*, American Psychological Association.

Turner, Colin, 1997, *The Eureka Principle: Alternative Thinking for Business and Personal Success*, Element Books.

van der Veer, Peter, 2001, *Imperial Encounters: Religion and Modernity in India and Britain*, Princeton University Press.

Vishvapani, 1994, 'Buddhism and the New Age', *Western Buddhist Review* 1 (December) (http://www.westernbuddhistreview.com/vol1/new_age.html).

Vitz, Paul, 1977, *Psychology as Religion: The Cult of Self Worship*, Lion.

Wallis, Roy, 1984, *The Elementary Forms of the New Religious Life*, Routledge.

Williams, Paul, 1989, *Mahayana Buddhism: The Doctrinal Foundations*, Routledge.

Woodhead, Linda, and Paul Heelas (eds), 2000, *Religion in Modern Times: An Interpretive Anthology*, Blackwells.

Wright, Andres, 2000, *Spirituality and Education*, Routledge-Falmer.

Yarnall, Thomas F., 2003, 'Engaged Buddhism New and Improved? Made in the USA of Asian Materials', in C. Queen, C. Prebish and D. Keown (eds), *Action Dharma: New Studies in Engaged Buddhism*, Routledge/Curzon.

Zohar, Danah, and Ian Marshall, 2001, *Spiritual Intelligence: The Ultimate Intelligence*, Bloomsbury.

Index